MONSTER TREES

MONSTER TREES

THE OBSCURE
POEMS OF HARRY PIM

Edited by
Stark Hunter

Copyright 2020 by Stark Hunter

Paperback ISBN: 978-1-63337-406-5
E-Book ISBN: 978-1-63337-407-2
LCCN: 2020912168

Published by Mind Tavern Books

All rights reserved. No part of this book may be reproduced or transmitted in any form or by any means, electronic or mechanical, including photocopying, recording, or by any information storage and retrieval system, without permission in writing from the copyright owners.

Cover photography by Stark Hunter

Prelude to the Obscure Poems of Harry Pim

These poem-children were conceived inside the mind of obscure poet, Harry Pim, in late 2019 and early 2020. I had the pleasure of encountering this odd and very old artist during Labor Day weekend in the foothills and esoteric canyons east of Santa Maria, California, at the home of poet, D. Lee. As a neighbor with aspirations of genuine congeniality, Pim made it easy for us to become acquainted with his life's-compass, and his staid past. So with fervent deliberations under the influence of various and sundry wines and other organic protocols, these poems found a starting point.

Born in 1913 in Wigan, England, Pim worked for years as an electrician's assistant in the oil fields of Santa Fe Springs and Fellows, California. Before that, he spent decades riding the Canadian rails as a fireman. On the side, however, this indefatigable, and still living artist, has produced a trove of obscure but fascinating poetry. At age 107 and still counting, Pim has, it seems, broken all records for longevity and madness. His secret? According to Pim, a terrible diet of constant greasy foods, a daily imbibing of his home-made, black syrupy beer (even thicker than Turkish coffee), and his ever-smoking pipe filled with sativa bud, are the reasons he has not yet said hello to, as T. S. Eliot described him, the "Eternal Footman."

While visiting with this undead relic from the 20th Century last September, I realized this artist and his "breathing verse" stood out from any poet I had personally read for the past 50 years, including all the "giants." His candid approaches to the themes of death, religion and sex, ironically three realities this poet has not engaged in as of yet, caught my incredulous attention. And so, being suitably impressed with what I had read, I offered to edit and produce his work, this short volume, under my publishing aegis, Mind Tavern Books, entitled Monster Trees, thus submitted for your approval.

Stark Hunter, Editor
April 4, 2020

Table of Contents

PART ONE: POEMS FROM THE CAVE XI
    Interview with The Dead Boy –Raymond Mizsak 1
    A Poetic Interview with Nancy Clutter .4
    Interview with The Most Beautiful Suicide 8

PART TWO: AT THE THUNDERBIRD LODGE 13
    Redding Poem 1 "Oh Noisy Redding" 14
    Redding Poem 2 "Sacramento River WordScape". 15
    Redding Poem 3 "Ode To Nicolet Lane" 16
    Redding Poem 4 "Flying Down Interstate 5" 17
    Redding Poem 5 "October Visitation". 19

PART THREE: WORD MUSIC 21
    Word Requiem in D Minor 22
    Word Fantasy in F Sharp Minor (3 Movements). 24
    Still Life For Words In C Sharp Minor" 29
    Still Life For Words In G Major" 29
    Word Toccata In A Major" 30
    Word Quintet In E Minor" 31
    Word Painting In Black And White". .32
    WordScape Triptych 33

PART FOUR: THE COLD DOOR KNOBS 37
    The Cold Door Knobs 38
    1971 (Hey Dude) 42
    I Recall The Smell Of That Place. 44
    Funeral in 1963. 45
    To the Invisible Friend. 47
    Baptism in the Back Room. 49
    You Shifted Your Legs Only Once 50

The 36% Poem 51
In A Suburban Paradise 52
The Rendezvous 55
Georgie 55
The 42 Inch Hallway 57
One Brick At A Time 59
Midnight Song 60
As They Danced Incognito. 61

PART FIVE: MONSTER TREES 63
Conundrum 64
The Perfect Day. 64
If It Bleeds After Scratching It. 66
Your Eyes Are Like Magic Marbles 67
The Last Consummation. 68
Time To Cook The Rolls 69
Monster Trees. 71
Even The Lazy Lizard. 72
In The Darkened Foyer. 73
If Youse Guys 74
I Am Your Shadow 76
A Singular Presence. 77
Hey, I Am Over Here! 77
I Am Touched 78
Nihil Obstat 80
Under The Lampshades 81
On A White Stool 82
The Dry Dispatches 82
We Must Imbibe 83
Hippie's Lament 84
Midnight Appraisals 86

Machines With Madmen Groaning 86
Kansas Poem #4. 88
Born Of Spiritual Spasm 91
Five Nights On The Fifth Floor 92
Cathode Rays In The Darkness. 95
The Big Digs 96
No! I Am Not Lying To You. 98
Under Fronds Of Stars. 99
Truly I Cannot 100
The Shine Of Secret Love. 101
Despair Eats From A Cold Plate 102
Under The Stars In 1952. 102
It's Twine Time. 103
Ode To Survival 104
Last Night 106
Alas The Mind Chains 107
My Soul And The Stone Creatures 108
Nothing To Say 110
Mastications In One Movement. 111
That Day In '73 112
Short Poem For Two Eyes. 113
Ready To Crawl And Slither 114
Word Dalliance In Pale Gray 115
Promo Code 116
Walk With Me 117
Dancing Now, Praying Now 119
The Stars Know 119
Did You Learn Anything?. 120
Apocalypse Beans 123

ABOUT THE POET HARRY PIM 127

"I have found both freedom and safety in my madness; the freedom of loneliness and the safety from being understood, for those who understand us enslave something in us."

— Kahlil Gibran, The Madman

Part One

Poems from the Cave
The Poetic Interviews

*"I fell downward as a restless anchor would,
hurtling forever it seemed, when finally
the black deafening crunch of my body erupted
like the explosion of a dry bomb."*

"This is experimental writing. I am interviewing a dead person, the 17 year old boy who died at the Woodstock Music and Art Fair in Bethel, New York back in 1969. He was accidentally run over early on Saturday morning by a tractor while asleep in his sleeping bag. I have read from four different sources that there were two fatalities at Woodstock that weekend. Some others state that there were three deaths. Any way you stack it, though, 2-3 deaths out of a half million people is excellent odds for survival, except for this boy, named Raymond."

— Mr. Pim

Interview with The Dead Boy -Raymond Mizsak

So Raymond, do you know what happened to you? Why you died?

Yeah, I know what happened to me, man,
but I don't remember it happening,
Cause I was in my sleeping bag sleeping,
I never heard nothing that morning, except, wait,
I do remember some guys talking from the stage
saying good morning everyone, then all the sudden
I am hearing nothing.
Where I am now, you get to find out what happened to ya,
you know, when you croak.
Never thought I'd be run over by a freaking tractor, man!
Heard later a couple other dudes died there like me.
A big bummer in the summer.

So Raymond, where were you from before dying at Woodstock?

MONSTER TREES

I grew up in New Jersey in areas around Newark,
My house was always filled with music and dancing on the rug,
From Jim Lowe to Fats Domino to Buddy Holly,
then Elvis and Bobby Rydell, and Frankie Avalon
to Jimmy Charles and Ricky Nelson, man,
those were some kind of crazy great times for music!
But the best music was still to come!
Beatles and the Stones were rocking and knocking
inside my bedroom walls in 1965!
Then came the greatest, the Jimi Hendrix Experience,
the band I went to see at Woodstock!
But, he went last man, and...by then, damn!
I went to Woodstock, not to die, man,
but to hear the music of The Experience!
Instead I heard Sweetwater and Ravi Shankar,
while lying in the grass there, looking up at the stars.
Dig It! Like it was really really cool, man.
Like, I had a psychedelic experience, man!
I was with this chick named Prism and
We cried tears when Ravi played...
I can still hear him, man! Still hear him playing
that cool haunting music, as it soared winglike
way up high there, in the heavy air that night;
Think I saw my death coming before it happened, man!
Had some icebag from Prism as a sort of cocktail,
And then I saw a lot more than stars!
I saw gods in the millions coming out of the crowd
like electrified gnats in misery after a black rain.

Raymond, were you there when Richie Havens played?

HARRY PIM

Yeah man, I was there.
He was on stage playing his guitar like a madman.
It seemed like he'd play forever 'cause
Sweetwater couldn't get in! Too much freaking traffic!
But yeah, man, I saw him play.
Great guitar strumming on a few of those pieces.
Handsome Johnny, that's it!
I remember now, he was playing Handsome Johnny
when I met this brown-eyed girl named Prism.
She had reefer,
so we went to the same field where I died,
and we smoked away my final night,
through Bert Sommer and Tim Hardin, until
Ravi Shankar took the stage with his sitar.

Any lessons to be learned in retrospect Raymond?

No man. No lessons to be learned at all!
Dude, look at me, I am a dead kid,
A dude who never grew up.
Never became a man or a father with a family,
Never found love with a girl or had a career.
I am eternally seventeen because
Some stoned idiot ran over me with his tractor
On a sunny Saturday morning in August of '69,
while I was sleeping, man!
No lessons learned at all!
Interview over now.

"This is another experimental writing, merging non-fiction prose with poetry; hence the "poetic interview." This is only art, and not meant to offend anyone's sensibilities."

— Mr. Pim

A Poetic Interview with Nancy Clutter

(This poetic interview is fictional and imaginary, and is based on 47 years of study and repeated readings relative to Truman Capote's novel, In Cold Blood, published in 1965).

An honor to speak with you, Nancy. Just four questions in this interview, and then, well, you will be released back to the eternal realm. My first question, and pardon me for limiting this discussion to that night, back in 1959, on the 15th of November, when you were murdered in your bed, upstairs in your room. Capote describes in his novel, In Cold Blood, your last moments, begging Perry Smith not to shoot you as he held a shotgun behind your head. Is that accurate, and how did you feel at that moment?

"It is all accurate, and I was terrified out of my mind!
All true, but wait, except for one little secret.
First let me say, no human being could possibly imagine
The complete fear I felt that night, my last one.
At first I thought it was all a big joke;
Wish it had been, instead of what happened to us.
But truth be known, funny how life is,
I actually liked my killer, can you imagine?
That's my secret. Wish I could have told Susan about that.
In school, ya know, we learned about irony
In all the stories we read for Language Arts.
So I guess it is a bit ironic that, well,

I liked the person who shot me in cold blood.
You know, the smaller guy, the dark looking one;
He kinda reminded me of James Dean or Marlon Brando,
With those black boots, the lisp, and the curl in his hair.
He and I chatted for about 10 to 15 minutes,
As he slowly tied me to my bed;
I think he wanted to talk to me though,
The way a lonely person tends to bend your ear.
We talked about horses and art, and college,
You know, stuff I liked.
He was a nice guy really.
Soft-spoken like a kid way younger than his age.
That's what I thought at the time,
But those black eyes of his, they were evil!
After he left me alone in my room,
I thought everything would be okay,
That they would leave us alive,
To be found in the morning by friends.
But the Devil visited that night, no doubt,
And that nice guy I had been talking to,
Now began marauding through our house
Like a crazy madman completely out of control,
Shooting my family each in the head with a shotgun;
My father first, then Kenyon, then ... well,
It is difficult, I'm sure you must realize..."

Yes, I am sure this is difficult for you, Nancy. Thank you for consenting to this interview. Do you wish to stop now?

"No, let's continue because it means a lot to you."

Thanks again. So, let's move to the next question. Capote tells us in his novel that Richard Hickock took you to your room and talked with you on your bed. What were your feelings and thoughts at that moment?

"Again, I was terrified of that creep.
I knew instantly what he had in mind.
It is true I asked him why he robbed people, and such,
And it is true he talked on about being an orphan as a child.
But my first impression of Richard was not a good one,
Nor did I believe his sad story, but luckily,
It was my ironic fortune at the moment
To be rescued by my eventual murderer,
From being raped by that creep with the weird eye.

My next question, Nancy, is what did you and your family talk about while locked inside the upstairs bathroom together while Perry Smith searched through your rooms?

"Although my father kept saying we'd be okay,
My mother kept crying, absolutely terrified.
We all were; my brother was literally shaking
And not because he was cold either;
So my father had us hold hands,
And we quietly said the Lord's Prayer.
It was to turn out to be our last moments together,
And I'm glad we spent that final time praying to our Lord."

One last question, Nancy. And you do not have to answer this. What would you like to say to Bobby and Susan after all these years?

"As Sue would say, 'Tell!'
And so to my best friend, I say,

I miss you, and Je t'aime.
Sue, it was awful. Just the worst.
Having to hear that shotgun go off twice,
Knowing my father and brother were being killed,
Then waiting, listening as their footsteps came up the stairs,
Pounding like my heartbeat was pounding, dreading
Shaking and praying, then begging my killer, No! Don't!
Sue, it was awful, but know this, I felt nothing. No pain.
One second I am looking at my bedroom wall, alive,
Then the next I am seeing a wall of light,
Beyond of which I am not permitted to describe.
Oh Sue, to ride horses with you again and be cool as fish,
Well, that would be just too good! Maybe later!
See you soon I hope, sweet Sue! But not too soon!
And to Bobby. I really don't know what to say to you,
Except maybe, thanks; thank you for offering your friendship to Sue,
During the tough times after my death.
Sorry also that the police picked on you as their main suspect at first.
But I miss you, Bobby. I saw you crying for me at Susan's,
I wanted you to know that, and to thank you with all my heart,
For being a wonderful boyfriend when we were teenagers.
I will always love you,
Bobby. Bye."

Thank you, Nancy.

Interview with The Most Beautiful Suicide

Evelyn Francis McHale - May 1, 1947

So Evelyn, yours is one of the most famous of suicides, since you chose to jump from the Empire State Building in 1947, landing on top of a black sedan, and then four minutes later, having your corpse photographed by Robert Wiles for Time Magazine. When did you come up with the idea of jumping from the Empire State Building? Do you remember anything about your suicide?

I suppose it behooves me to say something about it,
since I'm quite famously dead now, 70 years hence,
the moment I heard the rush of the death wind,
swishing by me like silver lightning,
I fell downward as a restless anchor would,
hurtling forever it seemed, when finally
the black deafening crunch of my body erupted
like the explosion of a dry bomb;
then I felt the eternity of instant death.
How is it then I could hear the voices of many astonished men,
men with trembling boney fingers pointing at my tranquil corpse?
This flight of a white scarf and my squished body,
had come to a sickening end, and I was the star for once,
draped like a passing movie princess in Barry's pearls!
And yes, I knew this would get attention,
having planned it all in tormented desperation,
while on the train to Penn Station that morning,
sitting and staring out that grimy window,
my depressed shaken mind sinking deeper and deeper,
as the city and my very life went by, forever
clicking over those imprisoning tracks,
for what seemed a lifetime of miles,

my tears concealed by a Lilly Dache' net,
then realizing reluctantly,
I could never marry the man.

Evelyn, in your suicide note you mentioned your father, and that you
had many of your mother's tendencies. Could you elaborate?

My mother was a depressed person,
A shrewish woman impossible to live with.
There were times in my youth
when she would scream bloody murder at us, her terrified children;
seven needy siblings in a small house in Washington D C.
Her sad days often led to angry nights with my father,
horrible screaming matches and uncontrolled cursings,
thrown about like hot potatoes with salted thorns.
I too showed a sad tendency as young as four years;
and as with most depressed souls in this world,
whether alive then or now,
no one knows of the private tortures endured by these afflicted.
No one can possibly know of our demons,
the same who told me repeatedly I was worthless;
and so, in 1947, I believed them.

Evelyn, talk about Barry Rhodes, your fiancé. What do you remember
of him?

What does one say after so many years?
Except, he was the only love of my life,
A love my shrill heart wanted no part of,
for his excessive love of me was the very stone
I ceased to desire, and instead of heaving it away,
I separated myself from it, and left it up there on the 86th floor,

with my folded coat, and a life lived in want of joy.
Barry was too fond of me, and although I saw
a bright future being married to him, I also saw
the upcoming years as his servant;
just a cleaning girl, and I would not endure this alive.
Before I left him that morning for the train,
he gave me a string of pearls,
and a June date for our nuptials;
then I kissed him goodbye,
knowing what my inner voice was saying to be true,
that I was not designed for this man's hand,
or his future child's needs.

A final question, Evelyn. Any regrets?

Not really.
Frankly, I am fine in this state of pre-resurrection.
It is preferable to working everyday, and being sad.
As requested in my final note,
I wanted no remembrances or funeral services for my remains,
and thankfully no grave in which to lay my smashed head,
only to be feasted upon by the earthworms of death.
Now my beautiful dust travels with the wind
like dandelion seeds in search of sunlit earth,
finding forgetful solace amidst the skyscrapers and the landfills.
Must we continue this?
I am not entirely comfortable with this interview,
this curious asking of these personal questions.
Please, let me be dead and forgotten.
Ahh, but thanks to Mr. Wiles and his camera,
I still live on, though in silent protest,
not that my life had anything worth dying for, but

a photograph of my dead smashed corpse?
This is my legacy? Please!
Let us end this interview now.

Part Two

AT THE THUNDERBIRD LODGE
The Redding Poems

"This final journey to the rapids of my youth,
Where undead ghost boys still climb the rebar rungs,
Atop the old tower on the water's edge,
Still spit into the blue, slow-paced river below."

"I had an opportunity to visit Redding, California in 2019. Loved the visit, but not so much while staying at the iconic Thunderbird Lodge in downtown Redding, two blocks from the railroad depot, and right next to Highway 273 south, a main thoroughfare for big lumber trucks, not to mention all the other truck-like vehicles driving by, creating a maelstrom of noise. The noise lasted all day long and actually shook the room I was staying in. This and the following "Redding" poems are based on that one-day stay."

— Mr. Pim

Redding Poem 1

"Oh Noisy Redding"

There at the Thunderbird Lodge in downtown Redding,
I heard the gods screaming from steel axles with rubber
Claws, scratching the timeless asphalt streets with mayhem.
I heard the sirens from the mysterious distances on Market Street,
As monster machines hovered above with roaring determinations,
And the rumblings of the trucks shook the building I slept within,
Like a raging stampede of stallions, coming through the canyons,
In search of prairie grasses and the sap of a million pine trees.
Oh noisy Redding,
You finally drift to sleep in the late hours,
But your Kansas-like silences seared my soul with your plaintive noises,
Something you could have whispered perhaps, but were not inclined to try.
Then in the wee times at vulgar five o'clock, they come asunder again!
The madness machines with roaring engines about to explode like maniacs

On hyper-drugs, make their appearances with screeching brakes,
And grinding steel nerves and hydraulic sinews made of entwined madness;
And time stops, as we wonder what monster has arisen from its grave.
Oh you, detestable ghoul from the grave, why must you scream?
There at the Thunderbird Lodge in downtown Redding,
Oh noisy restless Redding,
You belch loudly as you drink to the new day, and to the last.
Oh Noisy Redding, your maniac trains rumble and massacre the silence
As your old streets grumble like something wanting to get up and dance,
Shaking old hips, as with the tremors of the deep land, the sacred land.

Redding Poem 2

"Sacramento River WordScape"

These descendent waters swim like mad lagoon fish,
Heading decidedly south with a fiery mindless turn,
Their cool liquid urgencies reaching to all sides enticing
The bosomy turning earth and its pectoral indecencies,
With an impotent power unknown to anyone alive now,
As watery signatures knife their way into the crestfallen sand bars,
Adrift in an ambiguous undertow of death-marked reticences;
Swimming and floating lazily as a red lily floats downstream,
Enveloped cooly in blue clarity, absorbed by diamond sureness,
These arching trees lapping inward the reeking salmon atoms,
As rippling currents of heaving hands and wild bone sneezes,

Salvage the unsalvageable, and a solitary blue bird
Jiggling a crimson ring, as it bobs upon its ascended perch.

Redding Poem 3

"Ode to Nicolet Lane"

There I saw green visions,
and a young boy of 9 years running by,
As I stood once again upon the aged asphalt.
Last time I stood there was 58 years hence;
I recall the sun was sinking
like a ship into a gray gloom it seemed,
and summer was breathing its last,
as 1961's national celebration
of labor and the getting of goods, commenced,
with the flaying and cooking of
pig, bovine and crackling fowl,
our thick smoke arose
like a geyser of giddy anticipation
of all things worth working for,
and worth dying for.
Our thoughts turned to the times
of slowing down the stringent clock,
of attempting to lasso in
the final minutes of faint freedom,
when beneficent windows will exhale at last,
issuing the perfumes of time and closure.

One's childhood never really dies,
when it is possible to return
to these old mind streets.

I turn on my heels and see
the green trees of Nicolet Lane,
continuing to give a widespread shade
58 years hence,
and I can see Tyke the ghost dog,
chasing yet another chevy impala down this road,
barking and yapping incessantly
at a pair of white-walled tires,
escaping once again this mad dog running amok!
And look. I see Time way down the lane there too,
limping along with a walking stick,
testing the sediment and the feel of autumn's touch.
We both know supper will soon be served yet again,
and we will exhale at last,
while unfolding our napkins
to receive the soup tureen.

Redding Poem 4

"Flying Down Interstate 5"

We departed Redding at 3:45,
In the dead of an October night.
Those tumultuous streets were morgues then,

MONSTER TREES

As we raced to the deserted Interstate 5,
Zooming across the snoozing Sacramento River,
Going at a constant speed of 85,
Passing the snoring cities of Red Bluff, Chico and Yuba City,
Slicing through the darkness of early morning,
With the tule fog scratching over the countryside,
Shrouding the distant lights like blinders on a roan.
One city after another, my speeding treads arriving
In dark sleepy Sacramento in two hours.
With the sun not waking yet, but stirring,
The internal beast passed Stockton as a blur in time,
With other speeding drivers merging onboard,
As insistent captains of their own landlocked ships.
Then looming before us, the San Joaquin canvass;
A devouring flatness five hundred miles long,
Of faraway farmlands sleeping overtime,
The majestic surreal banality of Central California,
Magnetizing us, hypnotizing us to the hastening flow,
Of southern currents and windy traipsings;
This caravan of one, this golden fueled protrusion,
Of the nomadic heartbeat; the inertly-moving soul search;
This final journey to the rapids of my youth,
Where undead ghost boys still climb the rebar rungs,
Atop the old tower on the water's edge,
Still spit into the blue, slow-paced river below.

Redding Poem 5

"October Visitation"

A peeking orange smear
Talked to the lad inside his head,
When he was eight and nine months,
On a breezy October twilight in 1960,
As the orange light told him silently,
To go to the river's edge behind the red house,
To go there and see what it wanted him to see.
Night's shawl of descending gray began its covering,
As the boy walked down the horse trail in the midst of chutes,
Volleying up green and yellow digesting rotting salmon,
With lurching trees swaying a little in the beckoning wind.
Upon the smooth stones he slowly trod in foreboding fear,
And there upon a large smooth stone he knelt,
Folding his hands as in preparation for the mysteries,
And then, the boy was compelled to gaze skyward with peering eyes,
And he saw it, a silvery flying thing, ethereal as sugar icing,
Hover above him, as the first stars exposed themselves like a pox,
And the lad prayed to this angel,
This otherworldly visitor from the Iam,
There incredibly seen, on an obscure river bank near Redding.

Part Three

WORD MUSIC

*"Our unique human voices swim now in cloudy rivers,
Like fish that have been thrown back after the hook,
Old dead friends haunt me as the stars outside,
Continue their eternal dust dances in the dark."*

"This piece was composed in about an hour of intense writing, at the Hour of the Wolf; Don't recall actually writing this. But I do know what the thing is about. Once again, an old, now-deceased, girlfriend haunts my poetic vision from 50 years ago."

— Mr. Pim

Word Requiem in D Minor

Hello.

Fancy meeting you here.
Last time we met like this?
That would be 1979, at Rio.
I remember we walked slowly
Up to the second floor balcony,
Of the overlooking science building,
Scanning with four eyes the big cemetery,
Set out beyond a mile or so to the southeast,
Spread out before us with its big green mouth,
Yawning voraciously with empty stomach,
And the chapel there, with bell tower and chimes,
Drawing in our eyes as we talked for the final time.

By the chapel there one can see a patch of lawn,
Translucent and pure verdant as the 'old garden' at sunset.
We stared at the patch obliviously that day
And talked on, sadly and ironically; We were at last
Engaged to the coming times of change and tragedy;
Engaged to other faces and voices we had not foreseen;
Then one of us died unexpectedly and is now buried out there,
Aside the chapel, within the patch of pure verdant green grass,

With the pulsating piercing strides of the bell tower and chimes,
Throttling the survivors with their insistent reminders of grief.
Remember? You died 5 years later in an explosion of loud fire.
Witnesses heard you screaming as death pulled you to its womb.
Then it was your turn to taste the flash of finality;
Your intended inexorable date with The Giver and Taker of all.

You know, I'm 68 years along now, and the older I get,
The less I care about how I smell, look and talk. You should see me.
My hair is gone! All those long black English strands, like snakes
In the thousands, you loved putting your fingers through,
especially in the darkness behind my closed locked door,
With one candle lit and spasming on the ascending book shelf,
With spritzed spirits of shadow flickering upon the ceiling,
And you, my artist and sitting subject, both, finding the sky treasures,
Inside the quiet-night concealments reserved for us in the old den,
Now treasured as gold chains and ivory boxes, these memories.

Is it time now for you to return?
Is the window of life open now for you to slip through the curtain?
Is there a phone number I can call when you are free?
Not even a postal address I can send a letter to for you to read?
Hey, I drove by your house recently and our tree is still standing,
Still bearing branches and leaves, and I'm sure our mark is still there,
Embedded with a knife our initials and "1969" into desiccated bark.

Goodbye

Word Fantasy in F Sharp Minor (3 Movements)

1

(Andante con moto)

Hey man. Take this.

I got it last night,
under a fractured street light,
with shattered pieces of clear glass, scattered
at the nexus of an obscure dark freeway offramp,
way down there in magical San Pedro by the river,
around 2 in the morning with a creeping fog
rolling in like silent smoke monsters wearing a cloud.

You know where, man,
way down by the sea there;
where the juicy fruit gum never comes off
the seagull-splattered sidewalks, next to the shoals;
where the pelicans of the blue exploding expanse,
set before us like an endless slate of black fear,
come to die their slow noble deaths,
in the killing surf of dread and desire.

Hey man, look. Do you see what I see?
"Oh honey please!"
I know now there is a rock n' roll heaven in the universe,
when I see a surefire dream girl like her,
walking on by with those leering laughing brown legs.
Legs that speak in tongues
the sacred holy epistles and

the mind-numbing sermons
of old men with deep eyes,
sitting under starched mitres
in the shuttered sanctuaries,
holding black thuribles burning
with sweet frankincense,
mere words written and forged
by fingerless prying minds
in cherry-red rooms with no windows
or a flat divan,
and spoken by featherless, lizard-like tongues
belonging to a set of adoring sainted eyes,
now gazing at a dead and bloody Jesus.

2

(Allegro non troppo)

Hey man, watch this.

"Ah, excuse me young lady.
We met before.
In fact, it was here at this same eatery,
maybe a fortnight ago.
You were sitting by yourself
wearing a blue muumuu,
over by the abalone shells on the far wall,
sipping a white whale"
(with red lips opened, and fastened eyes).
"I cannot resist your nubile charms, miss."
Every forced giggle,
Every muted laugh,

MONSTER TREES

that leaps from her mouth hole
is another ridiculous attempt
to see the underbelly of quick-moving love,
with all its attendant leanings and compressions.
(Now she is leaning in toward me, up close,
standing on one foot; her breasts saying hello)
"There is nothing on my mind, nothing deserving words, I mean."
(I figured she was 19 going on a virtuous 23,
with no baggage, secrets or vile addictions).

"Mind if I sit here and
consider the possibilities,
of perhaps, stealing an hour or two,
having a few drinks by the neon bellboy, then later,
lying next to you under the clean white sheets
of your beckoning bed,
rubbing this sweet turtle oil
on your silky smooth virginity?"
(I figured there were ghosts present because no one was talking).
"Perhaps you misunderstand.
I didn't mean to insinuate..."
(What was I supposed to say to her? Stop with this love-making?)

Stellar days and nights await you, miss,
as all connected sidewalks await the heat,
the midday fry of tar and booty under the all-knowing street lamp;
My sins stare at you like some creep from behind a darkened window.
My past days and nights still breathe and sometimes wheeze,
like ancient tortoises asleep under a shade tree,
dreaming there.

3

(Adagio un poco mosso)

Hey man, listen to this.

"Miss, why are you kneeling there with hands clasped?"
(My Catholic past taught me much about kneeling).
"Then we must pray together, here in this spiritual bay
with all these dead stained saints staring at us,
and light a candle for the redemption of all condemned souls,
and for the remission of a multitude of catholic sins."

Amidst such holy quietude
in this sealed sanctuary,
with the wind soloing above,
through the choir-sated eaves,
such masterpieces of muted female voices,
waft lazily in the distant shadowed rooms,
inside old creaking houses, ensconced
on Jackson Avenue, and Burnside Boulevard.
I saw you one night in the dim candlelight
through your yawning window,
unbeknownst to you and your audacious shadow,
standing in front of a dazed convex mirror,
flexing in a liquid sweat with melting green wax
running and cascading down fiery runnels, splashing
like birthing rain from the sweat of love's dabble.
You found measured intrigue, and private pleasure;
I found a new but tilted ground upon which to pivot,
for I saw many shooting stars in the Orion sky that night,
and a passing midnight parade of holy virgins with torches aflame.

(Holy Father above,
I indeed confess this sinful deed, and am beholden).
Outside in the oblivious gardens of eternal noon,
the embarrassed trees continue to look the other way.

Still Life for Words in C Sharp Minor

They strolled the shady avenues
under a noon sun in the summer,
smelling the emergent gardenia bulbs
spinning maniacally in their mastery;
so they gathered up the white flowers
with practiced deliberate fingers,
bringing them to their stuffy noses,
to breathe in their exhalations of perfume spice.
They ventured askew with unstated intent,
roused by infinite atoms within,
to an open screen door,
wherein they saw intense sunlit explosions,
filtering through as determined light creatures,
and pulled through moaning space
for a secret rendezvous,
a shady sojourn of weird curiosities,
enacted behind a single closed door,
and other astonishments never before seen,
much less imagined.

These invisible wisps have entered in now,
with their practiced rituals and protocols,
known only to the obscure and the crazy.
They seek to find a still darkness;
Instead, they receive a green carpet,
stretching from room to room,
with old worn furniture gawking,
leads them to the regal dining room where
a crystal chandelier made of dull glass
hangs limply from the pale ceiling.
And flashing cloudless before them,
a curtained-spreading window,
exposing for the both to see,
a wide angular swath,
of shimmering gardenia blossoms.

Still Life For Words in G Major

Our slippery searching years peel away,
From a central pulsating rind beating fast,
Which glistens like a deep sky beam of green fire,
Emitting unseen filaments with tiny balls of sap,
Crowning their peaks with a watery white bulb,
of time mixed with multitudes of naked mirrors;
Our unique human voices swim now in cloudy rivers
Like fish that have been thrown back after the hook,

Old dead friends haunt me as the stars outside
Continue their eternal dust dances in the dark,
They shake my hand as they manifest bodily,
With youthful stubborn ardor and unwrinkled skin,
To past minutes and forgotten hours,
Now digested like last night's roast left on the stove,
By dead friends now holding flowers in a sullen graveyard,
That big green obscenity splashed with naked sun,
Peeling away from the core, the central pulsating rind,
The inner turning eye of the subcutaneous heartbeat.

Word Toccata in A Major

Jaundiced '53 Cadillac in my sweetheart's carport.
She leaves the hole keys inside the empty fish bowl.
Hidden in her trunk are a set of golf clubs with knife wounds;
Her secret boyfriend with the purple tattoo of a face scar,
Recites from shotgunned memory the Love Song by Mister Eliot,
As my sweetheart bathes upstairs with a fleeting candle and Camay,
Pure white, and scented as eucalyptus breaths in the cooing moonlight.

Fevered '49 Commodore parked luridly in her back alley.
He retrieves the hole keys from within the empty fish bowl.
Hidden in her trunk are a brace of golf balls with black bruises;
Soon he will trudge through fairway greens in pursuit of exotic birds,
Reciting Prufrock with two young robins pecking seed before him.

Upstairs now, he relaxes in my sweetheart's bath with Camay and a gun,
Pure crimson, and scented as medusae bulbs in the screaming moonlight.

Word Quintet in E Minor

Too many tan hearses cruise down my street in 1963
Too many grieving souls cry shattered tears here.
Green throbbing lawns ruminate like grazing cows.
Red-bricked chimneys stand erect in the tall wind.

You and I have footsteps to take as we smell gladioli in 1968.
You look sporty wearing a white skirt and cashmere sweater.
I sit on a bench in the morning sun talking about rutabagas,
As you arrive holding a white tennis racquet made of catgut.

She and I grapple the monkey bars with orange drinks in 1962.
The green ocean of expansive grass lay beneath motionless as ice.
Thoughts of quiet summer shade subside into a lazy sun-drenched day.
Afternoon tides melt into the memory of days spent on a cool porch.

You and I are eating amidst the others as they talk trivialities in 1969.
You are sitting close to me wearing a tight-fitting dress with buttons in front.
We're eating veal cutlets with mashed potatoes under a hanging light pendant.
The traffic outside is oblivious of our plans to make out wildly after dessert.

Too many tan hearses drive away from my street in 1964.
Too many funerals for the quietly erudite and the boldly afraid.
Green carpeted graveyards yawn with ennui in their insistent desiccations.
Old men with canes totter over star-lit graves behind rusted barbed wire.

Word Painting In Black and White

Cubed ice dismantling the plank bridge with pliers
made of syrup spilled with a dash of grief and brawn
the reptilian doughboy mixes up another cosmic batch
of truth cookies designed to mislead with wishes of
the big power grab

all manifesting inside the largest
television set ever devised with a flat screen as big as
a flying saucer that has at last come down to earth
so large and compelling my eyes were sucked out of
my sockets for five seconds of blind purgatory

something I thought of as an impossibility
what with the moon landings in the last century and
all the heart transplants with a dozen doctors
dedicating a day of grueling hours with
silver forceps and scalpels designed to cut and close

as with all relationships between a tight skirt and a mustache
on the floor by a black vent kissing with fingers touching and

moans muffled by the hand of fear there on the green carpet
in a mad darkness by the black vent and the trees with lemons
invading from days and decades earlier

when young women found the tile smooth and electric
with sharp tingling sensations on naked nubile skin
rubbed down with cold creams made of fish skin and
crawling eyes ransacking a thousand anchored ships
with knives made of pearl by old pipe-smoking hippies
who make love all day with sprawling girls seeking hot thrills
inside gardens made of stone and bootleg love.

> This is designed to be a "Word Painting" Hence the words are the colors and the rhythms are the brush strokes. 24 lines divided into 3 stanzas.
>
> — Mr. Pim

WordScape Triptych

1

Coming from the Underworld as a ghost, just sauntering out of the depths like you did;
With all the rest of us just watching and wondering what you were going to say;
Tell us young Beatrice what shavings you encountered in your intrepid sojourns;

Regale us with splendid tales, and grand dishes with squid meat and fried barnacles;
Intrigue us with your newly-learned dances taught by dead men beneath the grasses.
Manipulate us with your pouting grimaces when sad phrases turn inward the head screws;
Sweet Beatrice, there is no relief or recourse from these exacting heart exercises;
These time-stopping surrenders to the moist touches of absolute skin arousals.

2

Please lovely Dulcinea, guide us to the far-away stones piled atop the ancient green expanses;
Where screaming armies once pondered mortality amidst the spreading proliferating weeds;
Soothe us with your tender eye gazes which shoot through the airy spaces with calm affinities;
Made immaculate with silent prayers and lifted legs around the shoulders of the nobilities.
Create us for your strange mansions and your strange universes made of chalk, and fingering fears;
These soothing squanderings of doubting time, and the strange splashings of forgetful mercies,
Made manifest with the urgings of the stones, and the apex gods with the sharp plastic crowns;
Please Dulcinea, sing to us with your tenor gyrations made of pickled stardust and squid meat.

3

And proffer for us, sweet sweet Laura, your lilting songs celebrating the recurring exhalations;
From the lips of bearded nomads coming like leopards across the squared-faced, death vistas;
Expose to us your battle-scarred appendages where bleeding arrows found the stringed lattices;
Reveal to us your arched spinal bridges which flatten and turn with the seeking wind shears;
Gather us, lovely Laura, to your immense home hidden in the spiral ferns for tea and secret games;
Teach us how to be present and aware of the artifices, as rendered woodenly by the blind gropers;
Yes, sweet sweet Laura, we are at your service, but finally, kill us, destroy and annihilate us,
With your slithering clandestine movements behind dripping tombstones in the snoring graveyards.

Part Four

THE COLD DOOR KNOBS
POEMS OF RETROSPECTION

*"I sat close to you shivering a little and asked why on a Sunday.
You smiled and said it was something between you and God.
I replied that I understood even though I did not understand."*

The Cold Door knobs

I.

I am sure there will be that profound moment in time
when the dog out back will stop its incessant yapping,
Its unrelenting impulse to belch out its interminable wails,
alas, to inform its annoyed master and owner,
of the lurking prowlers, and the street whores,
who are always seeking cold door knobs,
as they sniff around the premises like aging detectives,
while trying the handles with ball-like knuckles;
but even the dogs inside the dark and dingy interiors
know when not to yap, unlike the one presently finding
repetitious solace with its swishing tail upon the sun-burnt bricks
out back there, where an unnamed river flows unobtrusively by,
headfirst diligently into the accessible countryside,
where lonely people sit in the sad shade at noontime
with half-eaten somethings, wrapped in foil
with quivering garnishments and curious sidebars,
but the dogs do not care one iota for such culinary escapes,
as one might expect,
for they know that the tastiest feast is the one
that has already been eaten,
and now has returned from its stomach,
undigested, and immaculate.

II.

"But, shh, I have a secret to tell you;
it is hidden discreetly amongst the old urns;
Look, over there. Do you see it?

Take a few steps closer, don't be afraid.
It appears to be dangerous, but it isn't at all.
My mother used to warn me of its capacity to kill or maim,
but denial visited my mind, and rightly so.
Don't be scared into thinking its three eyes and three legs
are anything aberrational or contrary
to what we have grown accustomed to
in our short time here on this curious planet;
Yes, it is real, but it does not bite.
I don't think you should feed it though.
It only eats cold door knobs."

III.

Shall we continue this obscure jaunt down my garden path?
Shall we not stop a few times to breathe,
and take in the extensive views here?
Shall we then gather a myriad of lupine blooms to decorate our fountain,
our oasis by the brittled birch tree?
First time I saw you was in a memory of déjà vu;
We were moving through a long elbow of carpet,
with paintings of idyll street scenes on the white walls,
and I remember your footsteps were creaking the floorboards,
making little mousey squeaks as you tiptoed past the shower room,
the one with the deathly black tiles stretching across its length,
like dead snakes drying on a rack, and you were sitting on the floor there.
"Tell me your name. Who are you?
You must be new because, well, you have materialized yourself;
Most of my ghostly girlfriends walk the hall in spirit,
and frankly, those silver eyes of yours,

well, they remind me of cold door knobs."
You sat there alone in the darkness of a July twilight;
the orange sunset to the west reminding me of
huge fiery explosions going off continuously;
I sat down next to you on the carpet there, and
I knew then you were not human.

IV.

"Tell me your name. Who are you?"
So I presume you came from inside the walls of the death room,
the last one on the right after the turning elbow;
"Hey girl, look over there, look. That's the death room.
Go there and turn the stinging cold door knob;
Go in there and see the dead man on the bed,"
he's under the wool blanket,
placed there by the man's wife and brother;
but now it is time to load him up
for the dusty ride, the bumpy dusty ride to the far lake,
with no map or plan or eyes in which to see clearly,
"Yes miss, we can sit here and huddle ourselves with these undead people,
they are as desperate as lizards escaping the vipers;
they never look at you,
they choose to ignore any glance from our eyes;"

V.

Attired immodestly in a short sundress,
my ghost girl sits now in a strange chair,
with bare concise legs crossed like bronze swords in the sun,
revealing dangling toes made of cherry and white frosting.

"Who are you? Tell me your name."
And she takes another drink, and smiles,
throwing her hair back,
"Then clearly it is something I am not permitted to know,
this secret no one knows about you,
Look here, miss, into this old mirror,
hanging a century here, recalling the stubble lost,
and the pallor of the long dead,
Show us the book you want everyone to read,
but secretly have not read yourself;
go in there, ghost girl, just turn the cold door knob there,
and... shhh... tiptoe into the shadowy death room,
the last one on the right, at the end of the elbow.
Close the door behind you.

> "This piece was a recollection of a typical conversation with a hippie friend, which took place in Southern California back in the early 70's."
>
> – Mr. Pim

1971 (Hey Dude)

Hey dude, come in, come in.
Been a long time since we last smoked the peace pipe together.
Hey! I think it was during Hendrix's set in Bethel, dude!
Here, let me move these Rolling Stones out of the way.
and the Taco Bell wrappers... There. Dude, let's sit.
First, I need to change the record. Let me look here....hmm,
Iron Butterfly? Naw, too psychedelic. Blind Faith?
Naw, they're too much like Cream. And I'm tired of them.
Hey, how 'bout Led Zeppelin 3?... Naw, too new;
Ah! Let's hear some very mellow Traffic music. This is cool dude!
It's their second album...very trippy music...
Listening to this stuff makes me feel alright!...
Dude, Here you go. That hole there is like a carburetor;
Put your finger on it and draw in. Then, let go. Boom!
Dude! Welcome to the petrified forest, man!
Dude! I been kicking back here thinking about infinity, man.
My mind is constantly being blown thinking about how big the universe is.
Dude, we are so small, so infinitesimal, so minute,
in comparison to the absolute vastness of the universe.
Dude, here we are, riding on this huge ball of dirt,
turning through space at a thousand miles per hour,
and we aren't even feeling it as we speed along,
like it's not even happening, man!
You know, dude, we are so small, so very very small,

we're all just a very small part of this vast solar system
with these humongous planets circling this huge ball of fire,
which are all just a very small part of this humongous Milky Way galaxy,
which is just one of billions and billions of galaxies in the universe...
Man, it makes my mind bend!...
Here, this purple haze from Michoacán will seal the deal, dude...
I also been thinking about God, dude!
We are all so small; we are all like spiders, just spinning our webs...
in this humongous garden called life!
So I must ask Dude:
What is God? Who is God?
I will tell you what God is! I now know! Dude!
Are you ready to hear what God is? ...
Ice cream, dude! Ice cream!
Do you want some vanilla ice cream, dude?
I have a gallon in my freezer!
Think of the millions of people in the world right now,
the people of India, South America, Australia and even in Dinuba, California,
who at this very moment, this precise second in time and eternity,
are sitting there, eating vanilla ice cream.
Hey dude! Be right back!

I Recall the Smell of that Place

I recall the smell of that place.
It came from the small side cafeteria.
I ate there daily for two months of my young life;
From the heat of September 1959, to the chill of early November;
Just a freckled, hungry third grader at Bonneview Elementary,
There, in the outskirts of Redding, a short walk to the cold Sacramento.
Other boys and girls my age were standing in line, waiting
To receive their lunches on green plastic trays at the side window,
With three smiling ladies waving for us to move quietly forward.
The smell of that place was the same everyday, like my mother's kitchen.
It was the smell of serial casseroles, cheesy and heavy with boiled noodles.
It was the smell of restless postwar children working up a chance to scream at recess.
All of us, just a bunch of 9 year olds, staring at the coming 60's with no clue;
All together oblivious to the future roadkill to appear, down the highway a bit,
The tragic endless parade of body-bagged playmates from 1959,
Coming into Dover, draped and cradled in the triune colors of the Mother Republic,
My friends from Bonneview who were with me in line all those times,
Smelling the smell of that place; that small side cafeteria,
With the three smiling ladies, waving us kids to keep moving forward.

"My deep Catholic roots are evident in this very personal work. I spent a month working on this piece, and though some of the images I use in this poem of my Catholic youth are darkly ambivalent, I still hold the Catholic religion with deepest affection."

— Mr. Pim

Funeral in 1963

Beveled dusty cracked glass shielding Mother Mary enthroned,
Amidst flying angelic devotions atop whipped clouds of icy air,
Enslaved by an antique miracle made manifest in stained blood,
With silent invisible memorized prayers uttered in ancient Latin refrains,
Bowed before upright holy statues and a gold-encrusted grand altar,
He stood back-turned under a dead Jesus hiding his whispering sanctified face,
And the mysterious movements of his ten pious anointing fingers;
As with an airy fountain, he hosed Unction's graces to the stone seekers,
Bestowing divine mercies by sealed envelope and a black vestment,
The lofty partial indulgences, the immaculate plenary indulgences,
Abundantly delivered and received using withy baskets and black beads.
Hollow dry penances offered up in a confessing private darkness of sorrow,
Within the squeezing superior stares of the priestly knot and the white Alb,
Altar boys on knees beckoning the impulsive turning of the holy human heart;
The struggled speaking of final toxic words on a red bleeding gurney;
Unsaid rosaries and scapular penances finding rusted, grinding precisions;

Broken trust and scarred faith wilting within clay idols and bloody crosses.
There is imminent death in the still waiting, there is red agony without the pain.
Black funeral wallowing within the hushed bereaved church at noon tide in 1963,
Sunken gray corpse of a woman serene, reposing waxlike in her beige groping coffin;
Grieving-suited witnesses and black-devouring shades standing wooden in dreadful silence,
Wondering when it will be their turn, their moment, to jump from this terrified earth,
These undead survivors, these breathing refugees of Unction's graces,
Remembering now, their concealed matinee kissing games at the seedy Pillbox.

"This piece took 3 days to complete. I experimented with increasing the length of each line, averaging between 15 to 20 words per line. Old memories of a friend, now dead for 35 years, haunts my poetic vision once again."

— Mr. Pim

To the Invisible Friend

The dredging decades have floated by like drifting clouds in the beckoning western sky.
Hello dead friend of my distant youthful days under these erotic jacaranda blooms.
It is my firm hope that you are satisfied and settled inside your deep and cozy earthen confines.
We spent months hours and minutes tangled together in a passing parade of exquisite time.
We ate a plethora of flailing foods together inside the old quaint cafes in busy Uptown.
We talked unceasingly under whirring ceiling fans in the yellow eating breakfast rooms.
You and I drove in suspended romantic time down the Harbor lanes at prying midnight.
You pressed your tresses and closed your eyes upon my shoulder into the late kissing night.
What has happened to your young voice and your shy waves to me from the darkened distances?
We have moved away from each other in decades gone by like skiffs in a crescent watery breezeway.
We have left behind a thousand inter crossings and a hundred by crossings with suspended ecstasies.
So sorry that had to happen to you that morning in October when the sky hi jacked your future days.

Look to the west behind these eucalyptus trees that now cast long August shadows at twilight.
Look to the blue-laced north now and rest your tilted head upon my shoulder as it leans westward.
Sorry you're dead now as you sleep in your grassy bed of jealous roses and wailing wisteria.
Sorry I had to see your white-sheeted body on the evening news lying there amidst the tragic landscape.
But now dear dead ghost whose faraway voice I can still hear even now from talks in the old evenings.
Did we not take long strolls on old cracked sidewalks under a curious canopy of jacaranda blooms?
Did we not seek and grasp great silver moments in the green-drenched darkness of hot skin and tears?
You and I know of those secret dances with the music turned down low in the swallowing darkness.
You and I remember the long floating ride down the deserted boulevard at prowling midnight.
We were irresistibly falling in love with the idea that this sensual drama in the dark would never end.
Goodbye dear dead friend of my distant youthful days under these erotic jacaranda blooms.
It is my firm and final hope that we'll meet again outside your deep and cozy earthen confines.

Baptism in the Back Room

In the darkness with the window cracked a little,
Allowing benign air into the back room, where a
Naked couple sits huddled, breathing in the cool breeze with
Mahler music streaming out of two black speakers,
As a single candle flickers on the shelf above the needle.
You said you waited a long time for it to happen to you,
And you said you wanted it to occur on a Sunday night.
I sat close to you shivering a little and asked why on a Sunday.
You smiled and said it was something between you and God.
I replied that I understood even though I did not understand.
Why would a 19 year old brunette beauty want to lose it on a Sunday?
You said it had to do with being angry with Jesus, and I said "Fine."
Your bronze breasts were the first eyes I saw that comatose night,
As Mahler once again took up the baton to conduct his 5th.
I took you to the beige floor atop the shag empire with determined cadences,
And I felt as if there were nosey eyes staring through myriad holes in the walls,
As we groped behind a locked door seeking the pleasures of the blood,
The window in the back room cracked a little, and you said,
"Thank you Jesus."

You Shifted Your Legs Only Once

We were on that school bus,
a big yellow one with black letters on its sides,
spelling out Whittier Union, and you and I sat next to each other
talking, arguing and giggling, you not caring if someone told your boyfriend
about our larks aboard that bus, long ago in 1970,
while on a field trip with our psychology class to Pomona State Hospital,
aboard that big yellow bus filled with white kids from Whittier,
except you weren't white, you were Mexican,
and a beautiful one at that, with high cheek bones and
brown eyes complimenting your mischievous smile.
We had just met Ray, a microcephalic, inside the hospital
and his miniature head made us wonder how such things happen to people.
You were wearing your usual school dress that day,
and your brown smooth legs were crossed
as the bus careened down Highway 10 exceeding the speed limit,
past burgeoning towns with cars passing by at seventy five miles per hour.
And the young voices on the bus increased in loudness like a storm rising,
and you flirted with me like there was a chance we could get back together,
but, "what about your boyfriend?"
"Take me away from him," you pleaded.
Then a silence erupted like a firecracker of impossibility,
and you just sat looking out the window all the way back.
You shifted your legs only once.

The 36% Poem

I recall going to the stained-glass church as a child
and wishing the Jesus statue would move, that he would
just step down from that hanging cross and walk among us,
casting droplets of healing holy water with an silver ice cream
scooper.

Then the choir would begin singing with the heavenly virgin voices
of one hundred catholic schoolgirls, wearing plaid skirts with white
beanies,
emitting angelic sounds and crescendos not heard by most human ears,
nor conceived by any body of do-good thinkers or evil-doers alike.

And as their eyeful gazes ascended to the heavenly heights,
with their attendant intonations spiraling up like a musical tornado,
I remembered the first time, that precise moment of childlike humility
when, while on my knees in the purple darkness, I sought forgiveness
from a secret sinner, one with a relaxing smile and a calming voice.

As he forgave me my trespasses with the Sign of the Cross, and a blessing,
this conflicted man of someone's fake god, which resides with silent
giggles
inside the soul of corrupt mammon, told me to pray for my sinful life
from behind his dark foreboding window inside the confessional,
while mumbling ancient Latin words with loud forced breathing.

And once again there he was, Father Fitzpatrick, with holy purple stole,
watching a multitude of sinful children say with folded shaking hands,
ten thousand repeated rosaries for two millennia, and a day,
these rabid canonical dogs, dragging huge tarps caked with lust

across the convulsing mud flats of earth, because...because, well,
there was really nothing else to say or do, except pray about sinning.

I remember she was standing in a plaid skirt, waiting in line
by the confessional, this sweet-faced girl of sixteen years,
holding a daily Missal in hand staring into it, wondering intensely,
if God had a plan for her, a spiritual guidepost from which to proceed.
But Father Fitzpatrick, from within his dark purple web of forgiveness,
had other spiritual plans for her, as she silently prayed for a sign.
And now, a statue made of ivory, not of the Nazarene, but of a queen,
comes to life miraculously, and she floats ghost-like above the ground,
hovering over the staring congregation, who kneel open-mouthed
and dazed,
as she points to the lifeless Christ on his splintered detestable cross,
made of wood, clay and paint, saving the multitudes, the living and
the dead,
with three bloody nails, and a stabbing crown of killing thorns.

In A Suburban Paradise

I was to spend hours on my bed
writing short stories in 1967;
with my left leg dangling over the left side,
I sat on the right leg,
like I was some nosy bird nesting on a log,
watching life and its endless intrigues,
concerning a sad lonely woman
in a suburban paradise.

I would stare at the quaint white house next door,
the Barren home,
staid residence of John and Ann,
a quiet couple in their childless fifties;
He, who went to work in a pink Ford
carrying a black lunchbox;
She, who stayed home
wearing loose revealing smocks,
while painting mysterious pictures
under green stretching avocado branches
in their open backyard patio,
paved with red bricks.

I was to grow fond of brunette Ann,
as I secretly spied on her as any boy my age might,
and watched her create art,
but only from a curious safe distance
through the concealing aluminum screen
of my open bedroom window;
she, with upright easel, a dozen brushes, and
interesting gesticulating body movements,
while conversing in a low whisper
with either herself, or perhaps a ghostly lover.

And I, fifteen years old, and curious,
oh so curious, describing with pencil in one hand
and an open notebook set before me,
a lonely sad lady with brown curly hair named Ann,
as she painted with pointed strokes and flourishes,
dripping desperate paint upon a white loose smock,
and I wondered, oh, I was curious indeed,

as to what she was painting on her big white canvas,
and what bright sensational colors she might be using.

It was not until a few years later that
I found out what Ann had been creating in 1967;
Not paintings with color-laden flowers or trees,
but grim drab buildings filled with trauma;
Of a bout with metastatic breast cancer,
leaving Ann with a flat arid chest,
barely covered by the loose smocks she wore,
ripped smocks picturing drab flowers and trees;
Of private violent incidents with John,
who beat her with an old Navy hand,
which, five days a week in 1967,
carried a black lunchbox to work.

Years were to go by
after those curious artistic scenes next door,
and I have often thought about Ann.
Divorce and death followed eventually.
Their quaint white house stands mutely today
a half century later,
with the laconic oleanders out front bending a little,
in abject exhaustion toward the ancient street,
not willing to speak about the unspeakable;
those secret untold tales of pain and trauma,
done furtively with the back of an old Navy hand,
to the whispering fragile artist living next door,
in a suburban paradise.

The Rendezvous

He sat in a yellow chair
staring through an open window,
staring to the distant west with lights bobbing
in a shifting sea of emerging fog,
He saw thick black power lines
stretching across the trees out back,
Stretching and reaching like burned out vines
from one tilted tree to the next,
Upon which a fast rat scurried, absorbed
into the silent darkness of an avocado grove.
Pulsating jets fly overhead in the black lusting sky
of night and desire, of dancing slowly in the dark,
with piano music softly playing on a green stereo,
A girl kissing passionately,
wearing the threads of dark Damascus,
with hair curled and perfume applied,
ready for a man's hungry lips,
and a night of electric touches.

Georgie

His was a pudgy boyish countenance,
With rounded river eyes and an Alfalfa smile.
He wheezed like a sick tern with repeated asthma attacks,
Playing hard at the various outdoor games and chases,

Of our fleeting childhood years in the inhaling sun.
He perspired profusely in 1964 as he sat with beads of sweat which
Gathered like a water pox above his lips, all in a wheezing row.
Bespectacled Georgie was the curlicued, black-haired boy
who lived two houses up from ours; the one with the green hedge.
He wore converse sneakers, a white tee and blue denim, with
Thick black-framed glasses astride his chubby white face.

His was a temper not sought by anyone, including Elsie his mother.
Georgie was her little boy, but when angered, baseball bats went flying.
Curse words were screamed loudly with one's birth name questioned intensely.
Stones and large rocks were heaved at innocent windows and nearby statuary.
Baseballs were hurled at the heads of other little boys, with misses near and far.
Toy darts were skipped across baking sidewalks to the bare feet of his playmates,
Producing more loud voices shrieking in pain when the darts impaled their feet.
Oranges and lemons were rabidly picked for the purpose of pummeling one's nose;
But gentle mother Elsie loved her little Georgie, and his little blue inhaler.

Years and decades sailed by like lost boats in a starless harbor.
Little Georgie grew into a pudgy man with nothing changed except, the drugs.
Marijuana odors hovered like invisible swarms of masticating locusts,
Lurking above the silent brick houses of our street, with old Georgie lighting up.

With a pipe and a baggie in his pocket, my old friend gave up on his life.
He decided not to work, but to take aimless walks down deserted avenues;
Day after empty day he took his drifting strolls into a personal oblivion.
We subsequently lost contact in the ensuing decades, and I forgot about him.

Until recently... I found out...
Georgie's funeral took place 25 years ago at Rose Hills Cemetery.
Rest in piece old friend, old tormentor, with your little blue inhaler.

The 42 Inch Hallway

We're stepping along the musty hallway now.
I am taking us on a fast-moving memory ride;
A mind-bending groovy slide to 1965,
When Dylan music was seeping loudly like a germ,
Down the green-carpeted hallway of my youth, from
Within the record-filled yellow room of my older brother,
Keeper of a hundred LP records with covers picturing gods.

"Turn that music down!"
His mother is hollering down the hallway.
"Can't you play some Mario Lanza music instead?"
Now we hear the soothing voice of Vin Scully broadcasting,
Another Dodger game on KFI with Koufax on the mound;
Soon, another ad for Blatz Beer and Dual-Filter Tareyton.

Presently, another annoying pause for station identification.

"Shhh, peek inside there.
The green room on the right.
Do you see her?
Do you see a fat brunette woman?"
She is wallowing inside on the wide bed now,
Fanning herself in the stifling heat with the LA Times;
"Come on Maury! Steal that base," she bellows.
The crossword puzzle on page twenty six
Is filled out in cursive with a number 2 pencil.
Her bedside radio is blaring occasional static sounds
Mixed with ghost music from Mexico.

Turn left now forty-two inches into the third room,
The faded beige-walled room with dead hanging draperies,
And a broken-glassed window emitting dust creatures.
Look! They are flitting in the air like crazy ballerinas,
Dancing to Sonny and Cher with that oboe and the bells.
See the boy reading Mad magazine? Batman and Argosy?
See him play Dick Dale and the Del-Tones with a scratching needle?

Now his grandmother is screaming in the yellow room,
Yelling in pain, while writhing on the green-carpeted floor.
"Call the doctor right away! Phoebe has fallen and can't move!"
Sunny and the Sunglows are singing Talk to Me on a distant radio.
"Baba is going to die of a stroke! Get an ambulance now!"

But Art Baker is now on television speaking to us from
Television City in Hollywood; his voice as sweetly smooth as Bosco.
But he looks like a guy who might sell you a Buick from hell.
Whose footsteps do I now hear coming up from the dank basement?

Whose voice do I now hear proclaiming loudly,
The big discount sale at Leon Ames Ford in Encino?
It is the pipe-smoking ghost from Nova Scotia, who
Died in 1941, forty-two standard inches across the hallway.

Can you hear them, my friend?
The weeping whines from behind those doors?
The grieving wails for the dead grandmother?
The incredulous shrieks of shock of the dead grandfather?
The wafting refrains of a drunk Tennessee Ernie Ford
Singing baritone on a black and white TV screen:
Let Me Walk With Thee?
I do hear them still.

ONE BRICK AT A TIME

The boy shimmied like a determined squirrel
upward stretching reaching
for the ascending bricks of the chimney flue.
one brick at a time
one foot snugly ensconced
in its leveraged place
and then another toe-hold there
as he sat atop the roof
of the old rumpus room
out back amidst the ivy vines
and the palm frond towers

with an Old Gold Cigarette ad
affixed to the glass door
he saw his special friends again
gliding in the distant wind unseen
except by him, the boy who stood
watching the break-in up there
a square door the size of a house
opened masterfully and unbelievably
with fire and burgeoning smoke
and then it closed again
with a shifting cloud
concealing the In and Out Door
for all human souls ever created
from here to there, from now to then
they took him for a speck of human time
erasing his memory of all unknown encounters
until a later time
now

Midnight Song

"Did you think I would not visit you?
Did you think I could resist you?
I came here by the air, just landed,
and I was wondering,
Can I lay in for a week or two?
Denver is cold in the summer; imagine the winter.

My bags are on the door step.
Do you mind?"

In midnight whispers I heard her, now
She stands before me, unzipping,
Twenty-two years of practiced waiting,
Twisting In front of a black and white TV set, now
It is midnight and time to make nasty love,
Energetic bone-rubbing love in this naked darkness;.
And now I hear the sensual strains of Mahler's fourth,
As I ease her down to the shag floor, opening wide
Her smooth tan thighs, for the unmasking of a wildflower.

"Glad I dropped in tonight for this layover.
I cannot resist you and your blue-eyed charms.
Have you any meat to eat and wine to drink?
Any others like you somewhere in the back?
Los Angeles is hot in the winter, imagine the summer.
Can I leave my clothes on your bed?
Do you mind?"

As They Danced Incognito

From where I sat that night in 1971,
I could see in the distance south LA,
Lit up like grounded stars in black mud;
As a rude wind brushed up against me,

MONSTER TREES

I saw you wearing navy blue with black shoes.
You were at the Roxy with my best friend.
Making out in the back row with popcorn and ice.
Tears of rage filled the ego ducts for two dark hours.
Then Broten visited, sitting distant under crushed stars,
My young earth, shattered in haphazard fragments,
You flitted like a engorged fly away from me, and us,
Your silent watchings and downward betrayals then,
Killed whatever love-embraces connecting our moving souls,
Our bodies, always lying clenched and breathing in a tangle, your
Milk chocolate cupcakes set before me in the naked candlelight,
With salty, salivating tongue-lickings bringing you to rise in my arms.
We lay with spent emotions in the dark room with doors closed.
Now we exit the bricks and the mortar to spy on the seven sisters,
As they dance above incognito in the cold firmament of trackless time.
"I wish someday to go to sleep and not wake up in the morning."

Part Five

MONSTER TREES

*"Monster trees with long tentacled arms scoop up the night cats.
They reach for berries made of balsa wood and Melba toast;
They reach down from far distances seizing innocent souls crawling,
These ghost trees, floating as life clouds, through
memory and time."*

Conundrum

This confounding conundrum,
This continuing act of untying the pesky knots of existence,
This conniving, beating whirlwind of ever-swirling stresses,
Again served up on a plate mixed with legumes and angst,
Is taking all of us to the brink of aqueous insanity.
Life is eating at our gonads like a ravenous chigger,
And the madness of it all bites at our minds and hearts,
Leaving half dead infected people with terminal frowns.
We wake up every morning dreading the endless daily tasks,
The endless psycho-dramas concerning trivial insignificances,
The never-ending shuffles through the busy, hopeful turnstiles, to
Another turn of the page, another interminable trip to Magic City,
Where we all find our share of romantic nirvana dressed in grey suede.
But a dollar must be earned to pay the bill of the one who must pay his.
And so, we continue to breathe on reflexively and instinctively,
Like fat whales pulsing in a green bay.

The Perfect Day

I believe I lived the perfect day, the ideal greatest day,
A day awash in a sunlit brilliance unseen since the first blink of Eden,
A day as buoyant as time standing resolutely still in the cool zephyrs—
A rarified floating air, cleanly sterilized by a healing divine fire.

I can still smell that perfect, utterly resplendent day in 1966.
The sky was brilliant and blue like the face of a vain diamond,
Redolent of star blossoms brought to earth by armies of the unseen,
Their reaching arms uplifted and waving, with undulations of rosewood.

I can still feel the magical freedom of living fast and easy on that perfect day.
Laughing like a thankful child under a blue blanket of restored faith in goodness,
Drenched in the magnificent serenity of sun-lit air on that perfect day in April.

I can still remember like a dime what I did on that perfect pristine day,
A day dedicated to life and living, like all the other forgettable imperfect days,
Days fraught with sickness and confusion with bleached out emotions laid bare.
I opened the window that day, and let in the pure perfect air into my old room.
The perfect day came inside and reminded me of the imperfect days to follow.

I now hear dying children singing like spasmodic seraphim in the hurling sky,
Dancing out-of-control, their strange pirouettes amidst yellow and red mud puddles.
This perfect day has seen many shriveled faces in the musty cafes, drinking sadness from a cup,
Coming back from doctors appointments, and the usual haunts where many lights flash;

"Deciding the day is come to leave the old house, this old street, under this undying sun."
It is time now to tidy things up a bit, as this perfect day succumbs to its sealed climax.
I stare into a beveled mirror and see a vast universe of imperfection. Perfect chaos.
Perfect imperfections that cannot be perfected by any perfect day, any ideal greatest day.
I now see the Perfect day! It is but a wispy memory floating like a ghost cloud,
Unseen indeed, by the imperfect straw men and women of this perfect Earth!

If It Bleeds After Scratching It

If it bleeds after scratching it, then you went too far.
I see a parade of dead people walking by me in this old dream.
They are eating bananas and I recognize their faces as friends,
I hear their familiar voices, and I wish I can talk to them again.
Then, as if a switch is flipped they can speak through the veil.
They tell me of fantastic sights to behold after dying from earth.

If it cries in pain after stabbing it, then you went too far.
I see dead girls from my past walking by me in another dream.
They are naked on the floor in the back room darkness.
I hear the familiar music of Copland and Gershwin on a record player.

I see young bodies squirming in a vague grunting candlelight.
They move by me like floating temple dancers in the moonlight.

If it says nothing after screaming at it, then you went too far.
I see dead friends huddled on a sofa inside my old childhood house.
They are sitting like wooden statues listening to my mother play the organ.
My mother is pressing the pedals barefooted as she fingers the Anniversary Waltz,
And my dead friends clap as she looks at everyone for approval as she plays;
The ghost in the basement loves to waltz, and I can hear him dancing down there.

Your Eyes Are Like Magic Marbles

Your eyes are like magic marbles
made of blue sky madness,
they draw my sharpest senses inward
rendering me helpless to your red devouring lips,
which pucker with a blinding instinctive intensity,
as with silent snakes seeking a cooler ground,
hidden inside a hotbed of conniving bulrushes;
your perfumed presence bringing out deliriously
a powerful draw upon my protruding screaming loins,
as if you had stolen my lapping eyes and tongue unseen,
rendering them completely to the burgeoning sky beast,

that now swoops down with grasping talons of arousal;
as you sprawl before me with plumes of mad impulse;
we lie naked, moist and spent; two lovers embracing,
forgetting about time and trouble as living human beings.
Your eyes are like magic marbles.

The Last Consummation

Hello. Good evening. Nice to see you.
It is always good to have someone to talk to,
especially now in my waning years,
as Death is softly playing the piano in the next room.
The piece he is playing is nearly over.
I know this because I have lived a long time in the shadows.
I have talked to dying faces many times,
with the same quiet melodies playing in the background;
they are like old friends who never change.
They stay loyal and refuse to believe the lies being said about you.
They speak up for you on your behalf,
watching your back even when you're wrong.
Such apparitions do exist I am told,
as there are many who profess to have seen and known them.
But I have not known any such person, or melody.
They are mythical creatures that have thrived in a former age,
lassoed in by the Sun God for an afternoon's pleasure with tiny animals.
These eminent beings who will stand by you when all have departed;

these are the rare honest ones, the decidedly wise ones,
all proportioned with a gutsy backbone that is unbreakable,
durable as the dubious winter grass at solstice time,
and as honorable as one's bloodline amongst the masses,
Can you hear the million shouting voices?
They find deaf ears, and a million frozen stares,
in the last consummation.

Time To Cook the Rolls

"Honey, turn on the oven to 350; the movie is starting!"

Soupy Sales is kicking back with June Taylor at Studio 50.
He is flirting with her leggy dancers as they feed
A sniveling White Fang burnt popcorn and frankfurters,
From a very salty refreshment stand in Studio City,
Under a cracked bleating Tiffany lamp, made of styrofoam,
Where dazed girls receive their first pressings of lip gloss;
They kiss and touch other crazies, as exploding rock 'n roll music
Alights the night like a torch, setting fire to the universe-
The dry gulches of shuttered churches and open conga grilles,
Where young men sit alone, pondering Cadillacs and Fords,
With silver-streaked teeth and brass dicks seeking a carport.

"Come on honey...I love you! ... give me another chance...
It was just a one-time fling, a meaningless tumble in the dark."

MONSTER TREES

Elizabeth Taylor is in the Ford next to us looking bored and restless,
With saddle-shoes on a tassel, dangling like dead fish hanging,
From her angora mirror, as she eyes herself with desires and plans;
Mere conspiracies which hold no erect realizations in the offing,
Nor do they percolate at daybreak with burning cigarettes, and coffee
As nose-snorting hipster-kids slurp on straws made of plastic delights,
Inside a crowded bistro on 14th Street, adjacent the Village, with
Horny busboys working fast for tips coming from tourists with fat
Wallets and bored dispositions, seeking autographs from the fools.
Broderick Crawford is looking chipper today; his open grave searching
For a taco under the sun, a beer, and a Mexican woman to talk to.

"I hunt malicious criminals with my Buick Century, and a .45"

The rampant streets play symphonies of mindless violence,
With embalmed musicians tuning their instruments with knives,
Killing outright for oysters and craw daddies, hooked up to wires,
Sucking, licking, tip-toeing down shadowy hallways with them,
Scantly-attired ghost girls spasming uncontrollably with loud squeals,
While gasping men with flailing arms seek a last terrifying breath,
Jostling inside their Cadillacs and Fords made of steel casings,
Assembled by the once-living, but now finding a prolonged sleep,
Under old tinkling chandeliers with cobwebs dangling, festering,
Like diseased worms looking for the relief of a masticating fish.

And now,
Glenn Ford is stumbling down the street again,
Looking for his dead friends.

"Would somebody here kindly and mercifully inform him that
His rich and famous friends are all in a graveyard near Studio City,
Waving from grassy beds of worm meat, and liquid fertilizer?"

"Maybe it is time to cook the rolls, and watch the ending now."

Monster Trees

Monster trees reaching down through insane skies like spiders,
They see something coming in the green benign stretches,
We are the onion ring bearers wearing dark-day secrets.
We know what happens when bearded eyes shut tight,
When the dead wave from hearses designed for blind drivers,
As the hatchet girls crawl into the blast barges of mindless ropery,
Monster trees with long tentacled arms scoop up the night cats.
They reach for berries made of balsa wood and Melba toast;
They reach down from far distances seizing innocent souls crawling,
These ghost trees, floating as life clouds, through memory and time;
Through deserted forgotten neighborhoods with skeleton trellises.
We are the lettuce turners, the meat shredders, with raised hopeful fists.
Wearing chiffon camisoles made with Melba toast and dark-day secrets,
The hatchet girls raise lapping glasses of mad rum to the blast barges.

Even the Lazy Lizard

Even the lazy lizard knows when not to beg,
when not to emerge, from behind the hungry black rock of
another dying hand, hopelessly clutching the mysteries of
another sit-down, in the serene electric darkness;
all of us tangled into a morphed city of outrage and fear,
ensconced with a multitude of luminescent lost eyes,
these sad and despairing souls that found ironic lucidity
upon the shriveled faces of unspoken impulses,
singularly positioned, as with all flora and fauna,
inside the elevated cages of human degeneration.

Even the lazy lizard knows when to creep and lunge
when mere minutes mobilize to paralyze the go- systems,
of squirming spasms under neon determinations,
enveloped like dead moth-worms, spinning insanely,
caught inside the smelly dank-eaten vomit climes,
with lonely cemeteries looking for new souls to fill the holes.

Now we can see the living rescues, the dying kiss-off's,
designed to dodge the fastest of the sky dirigibles,
witless designs which know nothing about the dry tears
in old glass ashtrays, from the bowels of old Bullocks in 1942 Los
Angeles,
and the hand-coffins with red, lipstick-marked cigarette butts,
left there by aroused, perfumed women wearing white girdles;
middle-aged spinsters seeking pearled mirrors
inside the shadowy upstairs rooms amongst the statuary,
and other obscene lotions, laces and leather goods,
designed to conceal, expose, and hog-tie secret lovers.

Even the lazy lizard knows when to lunge into the marsh fire,
the incredible sea of burning, with dripping petals of licking flames,
scorching nothing, and then everything, as with a woman's thoughts,
broadcasting boldly, as the only voices in the Savoy firmament,
happy decompressions, with electric mornings of a rainy pain.

I lie flat on my bed and I see the lost dead people,
heaving their stilted silent voices behind a thousand closed doors,
locked in with grief-stricken resignations next to silent clocks,
that are, by transcendent instinct, deaf to complaints and alibis,
told by hatless compassionate killers with pleated pillows poised
to smother the floor lamps, and erase the rusty love-making episodes
you and I had together, once upon a time, all those unzipped decades ago.
Thanks for the larks, young lady, indeed. Maybe if the crusty clock
has anything nautical to say about this tragic comedy, then, well,
let it rant. I am done. Done as anything resembling a life lived.
Done with this wasted begging and lunging in the dark.
Done with writing this forgettable homage to all lazy lizards.

In the Darkened Foyer

There you are again.
Walking this darkened foyer, and that carpeted hallway,
Eyeing the sunken-eyed dancer who forgets she's not alive;
She's just passing by all the sickness of dissipated humanity,
Wrapped in a single walk, and a solitary stretcher,

With a squadron of crucifixes affixed to the skin tags,
Applied with holy powders on these ancient, prayer-eaten walls,
These never-ending white walls that stretch before us,
Telling stories of prolonged death spasms, and postponement,
Of human decline in the face of the hopeful ones,
And the healing ones, with shocked knowing grins,
And the comatose ones, who know when to at last wake up;
Wake up! I say to the dead ones, the digested ones, long interred!
Now is the time to move your monuments and your dirt.
Now is the time to complain to the clock, the cold twitching clock,
That now holds no eternal sway in either direction for you or me!
Or all the dead ones, lying over there on solitary stretchers,
Under white sheets, in the darkened foyer.

If Youse Guys

If youse guys knock on my door,
I ain't gonna answer it, no freaking way, man!
Youse could be Perry Smith and Dick Hickock standing there,
Holding a flashlight, a fishing knife, and a shotgun,
Thinking there's a safe in the house somewheres.
I know youse guys think I'm loaded,
And that youse would kill me for ma' money.
Not tonight Misters Perry and Dick!
I got two bus tickets to Barstow, and then
Into the American desert youse will walk,
with hitching, trembling thumbs stuck way out!

And if youse guys come driving up and offer me a ride,
I ain't gonna get in, no freaking way, man!
Youse could be Ted Bundy and John Wayne Gacy in there,
Gripping a lug wrench and a rubber tourniquet,
Thinking I'm jus' a soft target for your Polaroid camera.
Not today Misters Bundy and Gacy!
I gotta a tan V Dub, all gassed up for the long haul to Tacoma,
And then, into the American nightmare we will all go.

But if youse guys try to sell me a bill of goods,
I ain't gonna buy it, no freaking way, man!
Youse could be Vincenzo Peruggia, and Doris Payne sitting there,
Holding a bag made of sackcloth, and a hoodie,
Scheming to rid my bank account with a smile and a lie.
Not today Messers Vincenzo and Payne!
I gotta fast plane to catch to Monte Carlo and Paris,
And I ain't taking my diamonds or my Mona Lisa!

Sleep easy youse guys.
I ain't gonna say nothing nice 'bout any of youse.
All youse were just bad folk.
Glad youse is gone.

I Am Your Shadow

You literally crawl out of your bed before the sun has come up,
Stretching reluctantly, knowing it's another day on this island earth.
So you drag yourself to the john down the hallway a bit,
And urinate dutifully and automatically staring straight ahead,
With thoughts of coffee germinating behind vague-viewing eyes,
Which are not blinking due to not being fully cognizant
Of your inherent location in the universe at the moment.

But you move on in life anyway as if this morning ride
Is your last dance with the fickle sun rising strong outside,
Like a lantern-laden ship drawing nearer to port.
The mirror in your messy boudoir of silks and sarongs,
Reflects an exhausted young woman in need of repair,
For the hours of menial employment ahead for the day
Will perpetuate those lines, those creases of savage age.

But green money must be earned with a smile,
For the butcher will not give his meat freely, nor the potter his hands.
You scratch again the itch on your leg, the rash behind your knee,
And your customer buys two of each, and now
There is green money in your hands for the till.

The hour of sad afternoon arrives and it is time to find a thrill,
The day is swearing obscenities at you from behind open windows;
It is time to find boot-leg love on the run behind a garden trellis,
Maybe with a mustached stranger wearing blue suspenders?
Maybe with me your reliable shadow in a myriad of plodding walks at sunrise?

Maybe with death himself, as he offers his business card
Smiling with a carnation in his drooping lapel?

A Singular Presence

A singular presence among a throng of grass blade,
Green as worm blood, her marked grave devours dead air,
Like a convulsing snake slurping a rat's tail for dessert,
The breaths of ghost winds embrace a shuddering tree,
In numbing grief with robes made of hollyhock and bearded iris,
Her still cry is frozen in the icy prisons of vague remembrance,
Then a single flash of monarch orange astounds the mute witnesses,
As it flutters like a praying monk on fire, landing on drooping leaves,
And her name, etched upon the singular sun-dried tombstone,
Sends to the tranquil estuaries a roaring river of inconsolable tears,
And her awakened soul finds a respite at last in its rush to rise.

Hey, I'm Over Here!

Hey! I'm over here!
'Case you were wondering if I was okay, I am.
I have no friends now so no one is checking up on me,
And I'm fine with not having friends anymore;

MONSTER TREES

They're all dead now, or there is a great distance,
A vast distance, between the old times and the now times,
I can see them all though, my departed chums from back there,
I remember their distinctive faces and voices still,
In movements at the old places, busy with life at the crossroads.

But they're all gone away now and I am alone here.
But that's okay because there is no phoniness when I'm alone,
And the voices you hear are phantom friends conjured
From the clay of half a century ago, alive again smiling and youthful,
All in a long line stretched beyond Hoover Street's oleanders,
My ancient friends walking up to me with penetrating stares,
Wondering after so many years if I'm alive and if I'm okay.
And I am okay.
That long line of ghost friends has passed me by now, disappearing
Into a mental cloud still hovering in the blueness of my mind.
But hey! I'm over here!
'Case you were wondering.

I Am Touched

I am touched.
You came to me in spirit,
As it should be,
And though I can hear the steel rumblings
Of the outside neurotic world,
I can hear your silent ghost voice squealing there,

As with a trumpet pealing,
With gnashing heralds afoot;
We timorous pawns cover the ground
For a fool and a twit.
But you came to me in spirit,
What is it you want to say?

"There is no capacity here
For any real truth because the fools,
Are running the film sequences,
With a creative terror unmatched
Since the old epochs,
When the ignorant wrote fat empty volumes
To the darkness, and its bottomless chasms
Of pyrite doctrines,
Designed by more fleshed-out fools,
With noses bleeding of putrid malignancies,
To entrap the masses with lies
And determined deceptions.
There is no space here for anything remotely true,
As a mirage feeds
Nothing upon nothing, in the dry wind."

You came to me in spirit, so,
Am I touched? Did you steal
My drowsy and still mind
For an hour in the dark night,
And tattoo those words upon my soul
So that I could fearfully turn back?
I do not want this responsibility,
Oh spirit ghost, oh you with

Gray shoulders and red hemorrhaging earlobes,
Arrived back from the old epochs.
I am touched.

Nihil Obstat

What is this wave of floating currents,
Which enter the dark side streets
Like far-reaching rubbery tentacles?
It is your resigned reach for something
Infinitely beyond the staid and the shrill;
Your grasping of one moment in flexing time,
Your attempt to save a universe out of whack,
By donning your costume made of plastic fire,
With flashing sun medals signifying eminence.
What is this jaundiced atmosphere I inwardly sense
Within skinned temples made of bitter cortex,
Here in the bulrushes, wearing a feathered cap?
It is the silent pulse of a forest lacking an audible voice,
A meadow with green eyes that scratch the skies,
Looking to erode for all-time the blindness of hate.

Under the Lampshades

You are hurriedly racing your crazy Cadillac,
looking to squeeze in more time at the yoga salon,
and have a relaxing conversation under a set of palm trees out back,
with sandwiches of desire mixed with sardines and mustard;
this person you are racing to is the one
who knows the right buttons to push.

Is it time for another epoch of stranded conveniences,
required by society as solemnly as a funeral with no body?
We know there is a hidden pain not felt,
not until a rain of shredding years find their progressions captured,
inside old rooms down hallways of musty time,
with apparitions of giggling girls walking back and forth,
looking for aroused embraces in the burning night,
Come with me now, is there no time for lazy hours under lampshades,
after we gather up red nectarines at the Uptown faire?
We can gaze at the old faces and wonder if they knew anything.

But inside this 1956 Cadillac we all knew where the flashlights were hidden,
And we all knew where the silver keys to the pink hearse were located.
Shh, don't make a sound! Try not to make a clamor within these green tiles.
There are witch hazel bottles half full in the medicine cabinets, and
There are asbestos catchings in the dry rot, and ancient cobwebs
made of beard,
Collapsing here with us in this dead basement of cement and lost whispers.
Shhh, she is tiptoeing down the creaky steps now wearing brown skin;
My breath is taken away as with all spirits ascending upward face-first.

On A White Stool

You know there is no turning around,
no pausing in any way, because the path to the woods,
where the sky demons make their homes,
has been flooded by the blue rivers there,
which flow by like glaciers on fire,
with life clinging to the whims of God almighty,
we first saw the downcast stares of fear,
made while sitting straight-backed on a white stool,
your troth of insanity, your refusal to bend or talk,
but it keeps going forward, this life, that never ceases to teach,
never decides to open the windows
when the blustery news reaches forth
from the darkest place downstairs beneath the dry rot.

The Dry Dispatches

To the sullen cemetery in the sun we trudge,
No better place indeed to find memory's heartbeat,
and a plate of forgiveness inside its eating green gardens,
as human bones hypnotize the dry dispatches.
No, I cannot sit here and continue to listen to you.
You try my patience.
My wish is for me to find death fast,
In my sleep of life now, no sooner,

For I have found distinct closure for my life;
Indeed I have made my final peace with God,
And as I now sit facing the sunset of my days,
I am reminded of so many faces from old times,
Old moments with humans foolish and brazen, as most are,
In their fleshing hearts and in their breeched dramas.
Shh, I waited inside the back door for your lusty footsteps,
Waiting for your anxious moving shadow as you arrived barefooted,
And when I opened the peering door, you said nothing,
Just turned around to be unfastened and unzipped,
as most sane lovers do, and then I brought you to the floor.
And silently danced with you in the naked darkness of temerity.
Oh humans, foolish and brazen as you are!
I cannot seek death because I am dead now myself,
Just a sorry ghost roaming with the myrtles in the distance,
Long ago, before the now of today and the road of regret.

We Must Imbibe

We are such creatures, that in the mornings of our fixated lives,
We seek out the substance of smells, the realization of tastes,
Because we must imbibe, must partake in the salty offerings of Hestia,
For it is the need of distant atoms, invisible to our eyes as it should be,
That we all move forward using trusty appendages which begin to creak,
When latter days manifest the trying times of navigation with old legs.

I used to walk the old avenues under shady trees as a dreamful boy,
Always wondering if life gets better later on, and it did, I must say,
But only after offering up my life and teeth to a service of others,
Did life and its tendencies begin to connect in wonderfully predestined ways.

"For this piece, I assumed the character of someone much younger than my current age, and saltier than my current disposition. This person has no gender and no politics; they have been neutralized by life, and its quotidian events that never change."

— Mr. Pim

Hippie's Lament

And like, everyday it is the same,
you wake up to a nightmare world called earth, man,
and the people on the screens tell you what's real,
telling you this is real, and telling you that is fake, and
all this twisted stuff with blood, just smears the vision, man.
And as life in this crazy-ass asylum goes on, like,
it's gets more freaking out of control!
There's spilled blood and death in the streets,
and thieves by the thousands are running amok and taking everything!

All this crap can't be for real! Come on God! Are you kidding us?
Like, every day some new disaster befalls another human being somewhere,
Something completely out of their control happens to them, totally random!
And poof! They are taken out of here! Like, some huge spider grabs them! Hello!
And what's with all the cancer? It's like the Blob from 1957 eating us all up!
Didn't we put a few dudes on the moon, like half a century ago?
What is up with that? You'd think they'd find a cure for cancer by now,
But no! Someone somewhere is making a hell of a lot of green dough, managing diseases instead of curing them! What the hell! Let's face it!
There ain't gonna be no cure for nothing! This planet is too crowded, man!
And like, everyday it is the same.

"Poets worth their "salt" have a spiritual insight into all things: good and evil, life and death, and can tap into the "spirit realm." There is no law in the partaking of salt. Thus, salt has tastes that sometimes suits the desires of the palette, and sometimes makes bitter an expected taste that should have been sweet. I wrote this at the midnight hour, requiring 45 minutes."

— Mr. Pim

Midnight Appraisals

The overhead street lamp was our only illumination,
As night shielded our concealed touchings within the moment,
Yet we saw light in the eyes of the stars as they watched us,
Peering at lips pressing past eyelids in the shrouded darkness,
There was music inside the shadings, along with hot breathings,
Made for the late embracing hours of our youthful yearnings,
With astonished meanderings and midnight appraisals of young lickings,
We first saw the highlands of our explorations in the mindless kissings,
We first realized the apex of our desires in the brazen lovemakings,
With the closing of our minds and hearts, surrendering to the moment.

Machines With Madmen Groaning

Machines with madmen groaning above me at 10 thousand feet,
Grumbling and growling like maniac sky monsters slurping on bloody prey,

Those steel dragons of yore spewing fire and corpses into the excesses,
Like Rodan and Godzilla maiming each other in the frozen spasming countrysides,
Giant crazed beasts reciprocating the deafening overtures of contrived violences,
Contrived annihilations, a few math equations, and we have the Beast rising from the sea.

Here, pour me a glass of your backwashed spittle as it internalizes with basically nothing.
It's time to find the time to describe a time when clocks will rage on like crazed moon dancers,
When the girls on the boulevard were cool and accessible in their cruising flirtations.
When tanned nomads inside their cool cars found gliding nirvanas, and a bra strap,
Amidst the midnight milkshakes and the incredible nude conversations in the backseats of time.

Machines with motorized redundancies tap into the central eye where speed finds inertness.
Life can be found below the stage on the Thames, river of history, by the Black Friars on Coffee Street.
Incense-filled rooms lie mysteriously down a long gloomy walkway around the opaque tree line.

Ghosts of codgers and spillmen greet the toothless ladies with bloody knees and rotting finery,.
A young bard shakes the hands of broggers and yeomen with dripping quills and pig's blood.

Grind on young thespians! Read your antique lines, not forgetting your monologues dedicated to fear.
Grant that the music of the spheres above captures the relative major, with silent egresses to be heard.

"This is Kansas Poem #4, alluding to the novel, In Cold Blood, by Truman Capote."

— Mr. Pim

Kansas Poem #4

Hey Hoss, slow down there!
No need to go so fast. Besides,
I don't want to go
to where you're going, and
I don't want to be seen
to where you're heading.
Hey Hoss, please turn this
furious black thing around!
Kindly get me the hell out of here
before it's too late!
No, I don't wish to see
this row of blighted Chinese elms and dead leaves.
Nor hear the badly-sung songs
of lost love and wild regret.

And, I refuse to see
the bloody scratches of truth and beauty,
so scrumptiously etched
with long blades on those splattered bricks;
Embedded there for the duration,
like the gum under your table;
Enmeshed there as the garnished gemstones
of the myriad fountains in Kansas City,
Polished with grit, staid tenacity, and
the time-shorn murders in the wheat lands,
underground in the broad basements
of purple smoke and black blood,
of silent stealth movements
under bending eaves, and a watching moon.

No Hoss!, I don't want to go
to where you're going.
Sorry, but we seem
ineffably lost and sadly wandering,
like a couple of dusty dudes
groveling for the keys that match nothing.
No, I don't want to go
down that long Chinese lane. No!
Turn this furious thing around!
Here the people sit on long verandas and
watch the strangers come and go.
They might notice two dudes like us and
wonder what we're doing there.
Sometimes I can hear
a loud shrieking funeral going by on Highway 50.

And those same people are staring
at the two caskets, and recognizing us inside!

Hey Hoss, slow down there!
No need to go so fast! Besides,
Time is not naïve, and Its retching Uncle
has left many a lover in the shuttered room,
up there on the 2nd floor,
has poured many a shimmering glass,
and licked many a teeming spoon.

Hey Hoss, ever take a morning break
at Hartman's Café back in the day?
When the Clutters would drive by waving,
from inside their blue chevy impala, heading
to silent Garden City, and
the cold wind blowing unheard there.
If you drive this black furious thing
down that lane there,
you will see it.
It sits like an old cat in the sun,
going nowhere fast from its sealed post,
high upon these expansive wheat plains,
under this dark, brooding, blood-thirsty sun, and
an unforgiving watching moon.

Born of Spiritual Spasm

We can travel mindfully as with source light,
We can project our sullen spirits outward,
To a timeless harbinger, born of spiritual spasm,
Left invisibly on the shiny star of suburban Formica,
And now we are flying through the pull of the maelstrom,
Traversing cosmically toward a bristling bicuspid,
The standard source,
The standard ending point,
Where tired eyes find solace in the lateral moonlight,
Where trusted voices lend understanding in the sinewy shadows.

Asleep now as the Colorado dead,
Sleeping and sunken now in their timeless tombs,
Alive as the everlasting sleep, this girly sleep,
As it lurches like a ghost gazelle into the soft entrances,
Lunging and leaping into the dark, abandoned residences,
Coldly forgotten amidst the green serpentine vines,
We can sense the emerging timeless harbingers,
We can recognize the unending, standard sources,
Of the bristling bicuspids buried with the Colorado dead,
Sleeping and sunken now in the lateral moonlight.

Five Nights on the Fifth Floor

8 December

Names and monikers are just smokescreens for the feckless.
They hide like poachers in the mud, behind a fake title of hubris.
Nevertheless, I am Doctor Harry Pim, MD, PH.D, LL.D.
It is all pointless really, what with the hounds of imminent disintegration
Not exactly at bay. Nor would I want them to be.
Death does not scare me one iota, after all,
It is the rankest of bureaucracies.
And I realize large sums of money will need to be exchanged,
In order for the business of my burial to proceed,
For it is common knowledge that many dollars are required
To hire the expert hands proficient for such needful and,
I might add, ghastly services. "Here kind sir, are two hundred ducat.
Please use a nimble thumb when thumping my skull later, indeed."

9 December

Today's favorite patient concerned a young lass
With a significant infection on her white Irish gam.
Brazenly red-haired like a mythical dragon queen,
I took to her infection with a blade and a squeeze,
And it weren't long before the thing turned.
This lady with the absurd freckles covering her white lake of a face,
Paid me with jewelry I had never seen before in our past dealings.
A ring with no stone, just black smooth cat's eye, ground into a circle.
I said, "madam, is this the real thing here?
I beg, madam, but it bespeaks of a forgery."
Then says she, "shall I then pray for another infection?"

Her name being Lisa Kelly, a name I find pointless, indeed.
Her white gam, though, compelled my mind to wander significantly,
As I excised the yellow rank infection with my squeezing fingers.
As I squeezed and prodded and poked with phalanges dancing,
I thought of a romantic private dinner with this old child,
A mere girl with twin mountain peaks in a burgeoning valley,
Whose worried mother waited in the wings, pacing with head down,
Praying to her god for a hopeless miracle.

10 December

With victory fresh in my mind of having saved
The young daughter, Miss Kelly, from the door of imminent death,
I decided that I, Dr. Harry Pim, M.D. PH.D, LL.D
Would offer my professional services and beg permission,
Written within a fortnight to conduct a far-reaching research study,
Facilitating one Miss Lisa Kelly as my principal patient, here
At my exclusive research clinic with massive concentrations
On massage therapy fused with soothing salves and balms.
I then thusly determined to find out about this Irish girl, and
Discovered in her chart to be just a month past 17 years, and
Inside my mind, considering the latest techniques at my disposal,
She is at the perfect age for my important and vital research.
"So, sir," she said, "where do I sit, and what do you want me to do?"
For two hours I spoke to her heart as she groaned with pitched squeals.
"So sir," said she after, " what would you have me do now?
Inside this comfortable darkness? I am tired of these playing games."

11 December

Life rarely argues back, so while just breathing air here, I keep quiet.
For if the rolling stone gathers no moss as it should, and does,

Than the wheels of lucid thinking must continue to interminably turn;
Turn and roll forward like the incredible confluent rivers devouring all the land.
They know nothing except forward motion; My snaky fingers now begin to reach
As they attempt to poke through the membrane with trusted pliers and hacksaw,
White austere fingers, which have seen a thing or two, feeling up the anteriors;
"See, we have fogged up the windows, and now a boy is coming with a flashlight."
"Ooohh... don't stop baby, keep going, keep ...shhh, as the boys go by... shhh....shhh"
The Caprice shook unnoticed in the parking lot with the boy and his probing fingers,
Finding flesh in the dark shadows, young excited flesh made of sugar and ice.
"I remember that night with you, licking your salty skin, and kissing you deeply.

12 December

Living active fingers going through that door over there, and opening this window,
Dying tired fingers opening heavy drawers and bulging closets filled with nothing,
Just nothing things made of inconsequential accumulations of no great value.
She deliberately bends over reading a newspaper at the silent dining table,
Wearing a short skirt made of long brown Mexican legs, smooth as buttercream.

"I cannot stop this gyrating because life is awfully short and what else is there?"
"It says here, baby, that the life expectancy is now 83 years for a woman."
"So my dear, just how aged are you, as you lie there wearing absolutely nothing?"
"Tengo diecisiete años, ¿qué importa? Sé cómo hacer el amor por la tarde."
She then got on all fours and barked like a hound, as with all crazy girls,
Now she thrusts out her brown erect breasts in a force of extreme spasm.
Living active fingers find the keys to the pleasure doors; nothing else to do.
"Look at us," I said, "we are just lounging here like nothing. Just nothing."

Cathode Rays in the Darkness

Thelma Todd is on the Late Late Show,
Brought to the us by Kent cigarettes, which refines and
Refreshes with the exclusive Micronite Filter.
Her still tragic life in the steaming suburbs knows no past.
It is a sucking monster to which there are no survivors.
The holy TV in this house prays with its face on the floor,
Screaming its way through backyards under the parallel clotheslines,
Illuminating with cathode rays, the fragile test patterns of existence.

Lloyd Thaxton is on at 4 o'clock before the news.
Dressed in a Van Huesen shirt with skinny black tie,
He sashayes under those hanging dangling long plays,

Like a finger person jittering across the sea with magic shoes,
Igniting the twisting dance floor with blue-eyed soul.
He is the coolest of the phony-star dance mavens,
Lip syncing with panache and moving lips through album slits.
He ghost-dances now Slauson style to the beat of the dancing dead.

Baxter Ward chews through the nightly harbingers at 6,
Brought to us by Marx Toys; Do you have them all?
He sits behind an square jet black table with head pointed south;
The Great Garloo warns us to beware the Industrial Military Complex,
The insidious Cold War chatterings of Nikita and Jimmy Dodd;
But Baxter Ward assures us he will be there when the Iron Curtain falls;
When Thelma Todd mysteriously dies again in her Lincoln Convertible,
When Lloyd Thaxton lip syncs one last time Unchained Melody in Vietnamese.

The Big Digs

Jackie Kennedy wore white pearls that day,
the day she showed Charles Collingwood behind the wallpaper,
inside the Big Digs on Pennsylvania Avenue,
in sight of the sprawling green mall a mile away,
where the multitudes have trod to see the big slice,
the big burned-out piece of living struggling democracy;
indeed, those oaken doors were closed that long-ago day.

"... but we the people who own the place, remember too well
the ribald goings-on behind the concealing ferns and
the haunting Tiffany glass window panes back in the gilded times,
when the lumbering presence of Grover Cleveland appeared,
from behind his golden painting by Eastman in the long hall;
he with his young virginal bride, the buxom Francis Folsom,
dressed in stiff white satin with trimmed orange blossoms,
intersecting her curvaceous body with white laurel lacings,
cascading down like garlands belonging to the watching Vestals;
they dabbled in the blue place behind large, fan-like ferns
as her mother and their twenty-seven guests turned the other way,
only to see the tall white obelisk shimmering outside in the distant sunset,
a vision bound by a beauty frozen in wet kaleidoscope, with luxurious
square pieces of wedding cake encased in small satin boxes given
to the whispering guests staring at gold frames hanging by silver wires..."

Jackie Kennedy wore white pearls that day,
and smiled coyly at Charles Collingwood dressed in a staid suit,
sitting back in the blue place, imbibing red wine from a silver flask,
wondering what it would be like to share one pillow with Jackie,
one hour of private passion with delving eyes and lips poised,
to find indescribable human heartbeats racing like primordial bees,
loosed to the staid impulses born within this earthly temple made of grit,
this drapery-infused nest known as the Big Digs on Pennsylvania Avenue.

No! I Am Not Lying To You

No! I am not lying to you.
It seems Life's turnings here and now contain
Inauspicious shapes of endless goings and comings;
It seems Life's headwaters of the deep waxed well,
the great steward river, of cold sinew and intractability is
rushing backward through bloody tubes and rusty spires.
It seems Life's dead people have arisen, unbeknownst
to the living, from astonished graves in gaping graveyards.

No! I am not lying to you.
There was a time indeed when a human person like me,
could calmly sit across from a human person like you,
and the both of us could pleasurably redeem the consuming time with
eyeful silences and poised stares containing muted determinations;
something like destiny showing up and knocking on the door,
saying: "your pizza is here," and you open the door wearing only
stupid shades while reading with an ivory looking glass.

No! I am not lying to you.
There was a time when life was peacefully secure and placid,
back when the pleased and complacent skies seemed bluer,
safer than today's chemical shroud impregnated by ejaculating jets,
35 thousand feet above the mad wasteland of spiritual coma;
The pulling dying aimless road to wherever your body is traveling to,
Is now a long coursing road paved with the fallow stones of fear.

These bloody sunsets have a raspy roar heard only in the death pits,
The final hors d'oeuvres served with croutons and screaming dramas;
There is now no turning down the forgotten deserted side streets,

hidden by shady oleander trees wearing bonnets of poisonous fire.
No! I am not lying to you.

Under Fronds Of Stars

Private Beaver Clever was blown to bits on the Perfume River,
Never having a chance to send that last letter to his mother,
The pearl-necked June Clever, dutiful wife to Ward Clever,
Mother of Wallace, now dusting her spotless house barefooted,
Before the golf-playing Ward arrives to solve all the day's problems,
And to tell him of the little mishap with the Beaver in Hue City.

Now unlocking the back door for Ward, June is in a whirlwind,
Rushing to get the roast into the oven so as to have some down time,
Some June Cleaver time, in her scrubbed tub upstairs with her white
Spotless pearls hanging, drooping and looping downward,
Magnificently, in black and white acetate, her perfect worried grin,
The grin which says: "Ward, I am worried about the Beaver."

Now Eddie Haskell barges in searching for Wallace and Clarence,
Only to gaze upon the white naked walls of an empty broken heart.
"Excuse me Mrs. Clever. My but you look beautiful today as usual:"
"Thank you Eddie. As you can see I am not dressed."
"I heard about the little fellow getting blown to bits in 'Nam.
I am awfully sorry Mrs Clever. I am sure he is in a better place now."
"Thank you Eddie. That is sweet. Mind handing me my towel?"
"Of course Mrs. Clever. Happy to help at this inauspicious time."

Ward Clever weeps as the cemetery-draped casket travels past
To the eternal moon, under fronds of stars above the Perfume River.
He now receives the folded Betsy Ross as the Beaver is loosed
Dust-wise into the bowels of insane pride and faithless arrogance.
Now coming downstairs the ghost of the Beaver gets his lunchbox,
As Wallace gives him his baseball cap, extending a final goodbye
to 1959,
To Ward and June Clever, forever waiting at the foot of the stairs,
Bidding the boys off for another sunny day at Grant Avenue Elementary.

Truly I Cannot

Truly I cannot surpass
this serene soul ride with you,
your quiet-eye caresses, like petals
of the primrose, falling from calm gusts
after a rain, disclose in the stars my hand
to grasp the hidden stone contained within.
I am convinced there are steep canyons
in your soul, as I turn the brass key
to our door of private delights,
our paradise so exciting,
so shattering to the touch,
we can bear no more.
In your face there is an astonishing peace,

So intense, so fragrant of love's perfume,
I wonder if it is possible to breathe again.

The Shine Of Secret Love

In the ensuing evening of low-moon time,
I am continually astonished at the rate of the dying.
What has happened to these endless dead,
These unliving shadows dressed in ripe memory?
Such sentient moments spent in a haze
nailed to the wall,
Such ancient voices still speaking of vanished lives,
Of obscure conversations in the old morning hours.
These dead souls still know the
turns and the names of the ancient avenues;
I can see their faces again and
hear their familiar voices in the coughing fog,
We can sit here in this darkness and
Leer at the lascivious naked moon,
Strutting up there, looking for the shine of secret love.
Or we can walk this slow avenue holding hands,
Maybe find the Life Stone of our lives and heartbeats.
Maybe we can stand under this curious streetlamp and
Kiss for an hour.

Despair Eats From A Cold Plate

Despair eats from a cold plate
It knows nothing except to fill its belly
In this never-ending jaunt to Morden Lane
Stenhouse Street and Swanscombe Road
Drop another dollar bill on the counter
Watch the waitress bend down to get it
She writes on a tablet her phone number
I call her when the sun is setting on Tuesday
We meet for wine and cheese at a side café
We stroll on Gunster Road and Haven Mews
She puts her arm through mine and giggles
She says there are brown roaches in the kitchen
A couch made of Naugahyde sits in the moonlight
Discarded shoes and intimate detritus scattered
Snoring lovers under a soft blanket in the darkness
Despair continues to eat from a cold plate

Under the Stars in 1952

Have a sit, honey
This '52 Nash Rambler of mine has gargled twice
It is our magic carpet to the peeping stars
Our love bucket flying high above the pouting clouds
Over all these blinking flashes and red-lighted stops
You are dolled up with scented lace trappings

Ready to dance a little, ready to make love a little
We will cruise a dark road listening to Johnny Ray
We will park alone by the lake to find the Seven Sisters
We will seek electric kisses stuck to shiny chrome buttons
You are looking like a girl on fire in that red lipstick
You are shaking my male tree sitting in that short skirt
I now take your pursed lips and apply my forgotten name
Take a breath, honey
Relax
It is time to dance a little
Time to sit back under these leering stars
Time to embrace now while time has stopped
While Life still has a living breath to breathe.

It's Twine Time!

(to Alvin Cash)

It's twine time!
ooh, ah, ooh, ah, ooh, ah!
It's time to twine, baby!
Time to forget about it all!
The latest lollipop disasters,
The catastrophes dressed in nude attire,
The latest bristlecone attacks
Manufactured with iced fear,
Riveted with barbecued bullets.

Lookin' good, baby; have mercy!
It's twine time!
Passing grooving styling peeps
Living lives in psychotic bondage
To the ghost children, still
Living fast episodes of ennui with
All the random traumas,
Passing all the purple bruises,
The red-stained tears.

It's twine time, baby!
The far-out space girls
dressed in sheepskin adornments,
Intense as roadside bombs,
Made of acrimony and glycerin.
Yeah! Them that are wearing
Dancing boots made of twine!
It's twine time, baby!
Ooh, ah, ooh, ah ooh ah!

Ode To Survival

As I sit here in this still cemetery
facing nomadic west,
Under these ancient oaks with
deep green leaves descending,
I see the ghostly dead before me

rising up as star zephyrs,
The men and women that once spoke
a multitude of living words,
Once strolled a lifetime of miles with
quiet footsteps unheard,
Through effulgent gardens of
copper rose and mountain laurel.

They come now with feet of
dust upon the mossy tombstones,
Human beings from the old times
now vanished like the grass,
They that spoke of the stories of
success, survival and tragedy,
They that woke at eternal sunrise
to once again stare into a mirror,
To once again see an aging face with
ageless eyes staring back,
These past human beings,
opening and closing a thousand grunting doors.
These blinking apparitions,
caressing and embracing a well of heartbeats.

Where they once sat and talked
on summer afternoons remains unknown.
Where they found accepting love
on dizzy evenings remains uncertain.
Now they exit the cemetery gate
waving condolences to the fearful living.
They whisper prayers and invocations
to the cedars and the lilting lilacs;
Whisper entreaties and supplications

never recited before, never heard before,
Now they lumber by me with
frozen knowing grins and nodding fingers.
I recognize their unsmiling faces from
old linen postcards in sifting time.
I now continue to sit here in
this still cemetery facing nomadic west.
Under these ancient oaks with
boughs of deep green leaves descending.

Last Night

Look up there.
Do you see the seven sisters?
The night is unusually warm.
I hear speeding cars going down Broadway.
The freight train is screeching across Canobie.
Purple-blooming jacarandas cry petals of rejection.
You sat on the curb and told me it was over.
Told me you were now seeing Bob from work.
I am happy for you if that is important to you.
I am happy he pleases you sexually when I could not.

Look up there.
I see the seven sisters dancing like queen stars.
Dancing stationary as with stones set in black marble.
You and I are through now.

No more naked romps in the dark den at midnight.
The candle is lit there and Mahler music still plays.
But vacant now are your gentle taps on my back door.
Missing now is the dark-skinned 19-year-old lady I desire.
Late at night now I lie on the shag carpet waiting,
Hopelessly waiting for your midnight tapping on my door.
But you never show up although you gave me hope.
Is it really finished? Last night
I fell asleep there as Mahler's fourth symphony played on.
I dreamed of you sleeping naked by my side.

Alas The Mind Chains

Alas the mind chains
they link up mankind like a mad ape
it pouts with empty paws
It never gives the past a second wink
never lets it push your guts out
we star freaks can carve up the sky
with only our thumbs
Then we can remove our belts
for the stretching of hide time
when you and I can indulge in a new religion
one that can grab every neon weakness
and throttle it into a new spasm
a new shuddering with zippers down and TV screens
belching out black and white episodes

of human madness minus a toilet
"you know what I mean, come on, honey
Ah, why don't we step into my dream for a quick dance"
a quick jerk then the Watusi and the Freddie with
bongo hands on sexy pleated pillows
lying spread out like dead crabs after the tide
this oozing rush of green life made of God's spittle
you and I can now enter heaven with skin cream
laced with peppermint, your warm hand
jerking familiar scenes from a James Bond matinee in 1965
this time there is no fiction
no revisions or retractions
just your lips against mine, your bone against mine
your tongue finding heaven in saliva wine
warm as the summer day
before supper under the tall trees

My Soul And The Stone Creatures

I

I can play the piano play it
In such a charming and disturbing way
That one-eyed monsters from hell are conjured
Beckoned magically from the bottomless mosh pit
My loud arpeggios slapping the windows with beast music
Bringing a stony rain made of dark funeral eyes to bear

A two-ton grief stone quarried from temples of blood
My loud glissandos sharpening a thousand knives of glass
Ready for the breach and the private tea for two at three
Ready now to be a waning groaning poet with nothing to write
I see ghosts inside my brain swishing through old dusty rooms
My soul and the stone creatures there with the lapping eyes
Completely wrapping their drilling gazes with green twine
Entirely as it is into a blinding braid of mystical tensions
Such as they are and swallowed by a phalanx of female mouths

2

Do you hear my sonorous keyboard entreaties
Do you understand that I cannot breathe as you stay distant
Would you care to sit by me as I finger white ivories
I can see your long lustful looks in the old musty hallway
Your hairy arms are enfolded with questions about immortality
Sitting in an old armchair with pleated prearranged patterns
Only the hobknobbers seem to understand these strange sojourns
These crazed adventures with dimmed lamps uncovered
You have been with the curious boys the biting insatiable boys
Crawling Inside their locked towers sleeping on beds of willow
I have seen the bronze statues of living dead goddesses there
Standing naked and pointed their perfume-sweetened bodies
Twisting and spasming among silks and satins laying haphazardly
Behind candle-lit curtains of skin with the curious boys pouncing
Upon open encroachments in the slippery submitting darkness

Nothing To Say

There is nothing to say most of the time.
Nothing.
Except when the bloody dirt bombs go off,
mostly inside these shady cafés of busty tables,
dotting this watery cove like a string of ghost-like pearls,
where I walk every dreadful day with the missus,
traversing Savage Gardens west of Shinster Lane,
into this esoteric moth-eaten bistro made of brick stains,
known as the Temple Bar, strewn with women and
lost men, as with me, dressed in green thoughts and
twisted tweeds, I and the missus, sneezing again and
covered prudently with enveloping cloth coat,
enter therein to see a host of mouths chewing lettuce.
It can assuredly be said that, by all accounts well known,
I seriously delight in seeing all my erstwhile friends here,
Carousing like old sea birds bereft of fond feathers,
regaled in permutations of sequined coconut water,
served by shivering island girls inside gourds of Mexican rum.
They come up to me now with long fingers extending upward;
as with pilgrims dancing in primitive circles to their god;
they hold up the low ceilings like Greek waiters with brooms,
as blind scorpion dudes dressed for love skitter about
insanely stinging our feet like a crazed army of killers.
I bend down now to receive your red naked lips in bed,
Knowing there is something incredibly noble in doing that.
Otherwise, as I shiver here, I have nothing to say.
Nothing.

Mastications In One Movement

Lathering on the ranch dressing,
mixed with honey mustard grunting;
these inhaling engorging souls are
finding the emotional precipice,
high up and dangling,
hanging by french fried ropes,
smothered in thousand island arrhythmias.
here come the fat waiters,
pushing arteriosclerotic meat carts,
spangled in barbecued thrombosis
and chocolate-covered infarctions,
served au jus on peanut butter trays
filled with maple syrup cherries and
white-creamed heart palpitations.

You know what I mean?
You've smelled those words before,
tasted their glazed cordials,
licked the candy flowers
as they swayed there, and
sucked the inner pap of the sweet melon
with perspiring brow; now
having a reason to wake up, it is
time for cupcakes and cinnamon churros
with the vanilla-skirted girls,
marinating inside bacon and lettuce taxis,
dipped in onion teriyaki, sizzling
delicious smoke with au gratin effusions.

That Day In '73

That day in '73 was as clear and pristine as glass ice,
Torched by a brace of smitten souls falling in love.
There was no lush music to be heard in this duet,
No swiveling rhythms or conga lines for the long dance,
Nay, these two lovers found quiet shade and a fantasy,
Parked intimately beneath a black walnut tree in August.
I saw the sun peeking at us through rustling green leaves.

You and I made constant eye contact and talked
Incessantly in the dallying breeze as the hours
Strutted forward like a striking drum beating silence.
Our eyes and mouths salivated with each salty utterance.
You talked with a Texas drawl showing white lusty teeth
As you sat cross legged showing bare brown gams,
Slender and shining as polished chrome on a new statue.

Who could have known then it would end up a naked failure,
A meteoric plunge from utter infatuation to the deep abyss of
Dysfunctional love, strangled by fiascos of precision and symmetry,
Of heightened expectations canceled in the sweating darkness,
The inability of breaching the sweetened walls, the ripe walls,
Of this nineteen year old mansion hidden below the tracks, with
This well-shaped Saturday night walking around with nothing on.

That day in '06 was as cold and overcast as icy black dirt,
Casting a pall of paralyzing grief the size of a granite temple;
There was subdued string music emanating from a boom box,
As the mother and her living sisters stepped up to see the body,

The sunken tan face that once spoke with a sultry Texas drawl,
Once lay naked in the breast-kissing darkness with eyes staring up;
Now the shining statue sleeps with Cancer there, being kissed again.

Short Poem For Two Eyes

Though this single clipped rose
has now lost its soul,
I know of a lonely hand
that would be happy to hold it.
I know of one I have not beheld
in decades of dusty time,
A red-lipped briar I once enfolded
with whispering fingers,
To feel its life pulse,
the smooth iridescence
of its stubborn rise;
To see its slow effervescent bending,
and then to see it open;
Alas, I am drawn inward
by its onslaught of invisible maneuvers;
By its unseen whip lashings
of the atoms and the universes.

Ready To Crawl and Slither

There is the annihilating
presence of something metallic
Two square feet from the spot
you are standing upon,
ready to crawl and slither,
like mindless spasms of red death.

There is nothing I can grasp
except your exceptional mind,
as it stretches out with a madness drink
concocted with desire,
made in hell by snide whispering gods
breathing sulfur roses,
as they gallop to stone meadows
pleading for a priestly fix.
We can walk now to the end
of this musty hallway and embrace there.
We can exchange fake names and
pretend to be interested,
or we can feign outright madness
with naked candles waxing out
oozing out wasted words and hours
with red lipstick and crossed legs.

There is the annihilating
presence of something quite ravenous,
quite ancient in its relentless trudgings
through old whispering hallways
with gawking gray paintings
of the stoned dead,

looking into mirrors as you stand there
exposing erogenous nipples,
erect as sweetened orange buds
dressed in virgin rags made of lavender;
I squint my eyes and I can see you out there,
ready to crawl and slither.

Word Dalliance in Pale Gray

Inside this pink room
you will find a pale dishrag, and the incessant
grinding of the death clock,
the insidious prefixed undermining,
of all human foundations set in iron soul.

We land-creatures instinctively understand,
the non-bacterial proclivities of mind space,
the incredible mundane bowel movements,
of monster spheres swimming in dust, spinning,
twirling like prodigious toy tops spun eons ago,
by invisible manipulating gesticulations.

We mud-squirmers begrudgingly acknowledge,
the duodenum-laced intricacies of naked bone time,
the interminable kowtowings and interfacings,
to the prince of absurdities and plastic grandeur,
to the remonstrances of a twisted nomenclature.

We big-bellied earth-squatters and day-dreamers,
incredulously deny the daily grindings of the death clock,
the incessant turning in circles inside this warm place,
this smooth pink room hidden by the secret machinations,
the esoteric connivings, of the mindless mud-squirmers,
and the round-eyed, flat-footed bone-crunchers,
performed adroitly with tinctured pond water
amidst a pale dishrag.

Promo Code

Your furious heart beats carnivorously.
It is coming apart with all the other lost trinkets.
It is being transported in a same-day delivery,
directly into your phony
living spaces of green death,
preening with diluted details
and tired touchings.

Upstairs, and down the dimly lit hallway
of cobweb anxieties and staring finger jabs,
two heartbeats walk, and a royal feel-out
behind a moaning locked door takes place;
It is the promo code for another
hiccup of tentative existence,
vibrating now on your dusty
console from a shuttered Sears,

displayed atop your cathode ray screen,
like a tombstone made of ice cream,
stretched out in a medieval coma,
scanning the underbelly for the promo code.

Oh you and your furious soul.
I remember your black pleading eyes,
your surrendering blood dance inside
the locked darkness of mad quixotic love,
your flesh-eating universe of
milky-sugared stars spurting wildly,
amidst the inner ancient attic lights,
as with a net cast from rocks high up,
by noble appendages of temporary elasticity-
this promo code for a quick exit, holding
dead flowers, strumming a blues guitar.

Walk With Me

Walk with me now down this extinct street from 1963,
This old breathing avenue now entirely disappeared,
Long ago bulldozed for a strip mall and a Shell station.
We were seriously young and searching for flesh back then.

Walk with me still as we find dead voices under heartsick trees,
Wondering when the ghost dreams might explode again,
When the freaks of fame might light another victory cigar,

As the death dancers gather more pale flowers at noon,
So we can see for ourselves the costumes of pyrite madness.

Walk with me still down this petrified street from 1963,
We will speak of love because it sounds so good to us, and
We'll listen to Sunny and the Sunglows, holding each other close;
Darling I love you as this earth moves and shakes; talk to me.

Walk with me now into these curious shops for ribbons and lace;
Candy-shaped as fried gemstones, with hearts bleeding blue love.
We will dance through the night in the presence of a single naked candle,
Hostage to Frank Sinatra, Artie Shaw, and our entangled pirouettes of
Cotton perfumed essences with soft fur of leopard, newly shaved;
We will lick red lips knowing it will taste good as we shudder in ecstasy..

Dancing Now, Praying Now

Sandwich-makers wearing black belts and blue bonnets,
Sharpen curated knives for the cutting ceremonies.
Dutch boy machinations conceived in the back seat;
A cadre of horny priests step to the altar under a ghost moon.
Spaz boys tattooed for the final hoedown from hell,
Seek the ballistic pleasures of the bullet and the bomb.
They know when to hang up the pink princess phone,
As Night without shame slowly strips to the ankles,
Dancing now with the faceless wind at her arching back.
Opioid freaks swallow dead things made of purple-skinned trauma,

Praying now for another night of lacerations and indulgences;
Here we are folks inside this cosmic petrie dish filled with fear,
Baking the beans of annihilating females wearing DNA earrings,
With drooping breast bombs dangling like ambivalent tangerines,
Wondering if Time ever shows up late for the decisive festivities.

THE STARS KNOW

The stars know our decided destiny.
They can hear our driveling deliberations.
They can see the welts on our arms,
Lacerated there by pill bugs dressed in fear.
Born aloft by evil shadows without eyes,
The stars are aware of the ghost voices,
Pleading again to steer clear the flatlands.
To find new passages through the barricades.
To remember familiar voices of the dead,
To visit their still tombstones in the high grasses.
The stars remember them like falling snow,
Like journeys from home to someone's heart.
They can feel the warm pulse of shuddering desire,
The electric touch of first love in the darkness.
The stars offer a toast of rum to the futile universe.
A genuflection of cancelled invocations at noontime.
They can smell the damp roses as they straddle time,
Take hostage the inner heart of the flower's mind.
The stars know my death day and choose to keep mum.

They know why I crossed and penetrated the inner skin.
They have decided to grant me their purple absolutions.

Did You Learn Anything?

Go ahead.
Put your shoes on.
Walk outside and face the nervous day.
Know that your lungs will not resist you.
Know that your heart will still stir.
Put the key in the ignition.
Now turn the crank.

You are back there now.
As if in a dream so ordered.
It is 1937 on Hoover Street.
The oleanders are bleeding.
Perfumed orange trees spit white loogies.
Clean children emerge from green digs.
Mothers hang clothes on uncomplaining lines.

Your wife is back there.
She's wearing black reptile oxfords.
Go ahead.
Walk down the long gravelly driveway.

Pass the back porch steps there.
Pass the red-blooming bougainvillea.
There she is, alive again as she was.
Unfurling laundry with old clothespins.
Singing an old Salvation Army song.
Go ahead.
Talk to her.
Tell her who you are.

"Baba. Baba, it's me,
Your surviving husband, Harry.
I wanted to tell you,
I am a poet now.
An engineer of the human soul.
A standard-bearer for the mad,
Dressed in mindful metaphor.
You look young despite the goiter,
There inside your sinewy neck.
It appears and seems as if,
The goiter is a python at sleep,
Scrunched up inside there,
All rolled up like kneaded bread.
I hope it doesn't hurt you.
I come from the future, Baba.
I know that sounds crazy, but
I am visiting from the year 2020."

The world of my time screams
In lockdown, like medieval Europe,

MONSTER TREES

People of every nation and tongue,
Too afraid to emerge from their walls,
Too fearful of even breathing in,
Imbibing in, with lost enthusiasms,
Mountain fresh air from the antipodes;
Fearful of catching and releasing It – the
Corona Virus monster microbe moving
Silently across the terrified landscapes,
Devouring the cool mornings,
Aside the neon evenings, even
Robbing the noon day of hopeful turnings.

"Baba, can I stay here with you,
In this golden simple time of 1937?
May I remain here now,
A happy and relieved rider,
Astride this awful depression horse?"

Go ahead.
It is time to return.
Baba died in 1963 and cannot hear you.
Turn the key off in the ignition.
You are back now where you belong.
It is 2020 in the United States of America.
Baba is sleeping in the graveyard now.
You are being held hostage by a germ.
Kick your shoes off now and think.
Did you learn anything?

Apocalypse Beans

Sometimes it seems
your chest is about to cave in.
You try to catch a breath but
your heart flutters like a dry leaf;
Just more suburban undulations;
Dressed down for a slow blues song.
Apocalypse Beans sizzle on the fire.

Life has such trying interludes,
when it seems you can't go further.
You are so tired and scared,
you can hardly urinate at dawn.
Your mind begins to see
air movies of the dead ascending;
Crawling out of cracked tombs
dressed sedately for the soirée.

A million funerals go by with
skeleton girls sucking on pixy stix.
Madness angels in garters pass over
sleeping streets searching for blood trees.
Stallion-dressed men-dogs chase down
old octogenarians for bones and wisdom teeth.

Fear worms from hell come slinking,
Oozing out of a million eye sockets,
Sucking blood and brains sifting
through transparent wires attached
to rubber-hosed machines in musty rooms.
A million funerals moan inside the old graveyard

MONSTER TREES

adjacent the First Methodist confines.
Gum-chewing embalmers gather
to sing a torch song to the driveling and the dying.

Sometimes it seems
I can hear the female choirs singing,
their high-pitched Latin refrains again.
They stand erect in the choir loft fingering missals.
The young girls up there,
wear choir togs and slithering plaid beanies.
They read the notes and eye the glowing boys below.
Jesus and the stained glass ghosts look up from earth.
Apocalypse Beans sizzle on the fire.
Their cackle reamed with burning forget-me-nots.

I Harry Pim attest on this day in April of 2020, with perspiry mind and stout heart, that the aforementioned and listed poetry was indeed written by my hand and mind, during the years of our Lord, September, 2019- March, 2020. -so therefore delared: I am Mr. Pim.

ABOUT THE POET
HARRY PIM

(Photo taken in 1937)

Mr. Pim did not attend or graduate from any prestigious or accredited university, nor was he the winner or recipient of any prestigious book prize or contest. Moreover, Mr. Pim has not worked under any acclaimed mentor with a Ph.d from Harvard or Yale, or any other poet or person with impressive academic credentials or prior publications. Mr. Pim has not been a part of any well-known internship or fellowship, nor has he belonged to any elite writing guild or poetry organization in his career. In essence, Mr. Pim is a bonafide nobody, completely unknown by all, both alive and dead. Monster Trees is his first work of poetry.

"There is no space here for anything remotely true,
As a mirage feeds
Nothing upon nothing, in the dry wind."

Harry Pim

2020

www.ingramcontent.com/pod-product-compliance
Lightning Source LLC
Chambersburg PA
CBHW032038040426
42449CB00007B/932